# *Steps i*
# UNDERSTANDING
# MATHEMATICS

## J. D. COLLINS (Editor)
## I. A. BROWN, C. J. COX
## J. R. MAGSON, M. C. TONKIN

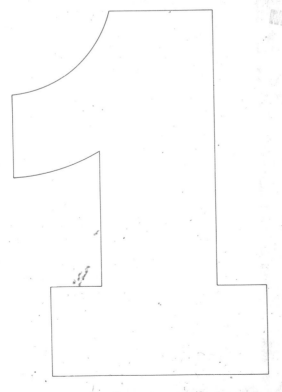

# JOHN MURRAY

# Acknowledgements

**Cover design** by Peter Theodosiou

**Diagrams** by Technical Art Services

**Cartoons** by Gwyneth Cook, Impress International

**Text layout** by Impress International

Photographs on pp. 19, 46, 52, 82 (bottom right), 96, 118, 142, 149 by David Purdie. Copyright photographs by permission of: CEGB (p.1), NHPA (p.82, top), ZEFA (p.82, bottom left), Cordon Art, Baarn, Holland, © 1988 M. C. Escher Heirs (p.97), Aerofilms (p.98), Transport and Road Research Laboratory (p.112, top), Salter (p.112, bottom left and right), Science Museum (p.152).

© J. D. Collins, I. Brown, C. Cox, J. Magson, M. Tonkin 1989

First published 1989
by John Murray (Publishers) Ltd
50 Albemarle Street, London W1X 4BD

Reprinted 1992, 1994, 1996

Printed in Great Britain by Alden, Oxford, Didcot and Northampton

British Library Cataloguing in Publication Data

Steps in understanding mathematics (SUM).
1. Mathematics – for schools
510

ISBN 0-7195-4450-5 Bk.1: Pupils'

# About this book

This is the first book of **Steps in Understanding Mathematics,**
a course leading to 14+ assessment and GCSE in Mathematics.

There are 29 chapters, divided into:

- **Points to discuss . . .** to give you the chance to talk about the
  mathematics, and to see how it links with everyday life.

- **Exercises or Projects** to give you practice at different kinds
  of questions and skills, and to help you improve your understanding of the mathematics.

- **Extension work** (boxed) at the end of some exercises to give
  you a challenge with harder problems.

New ideas and words are clearly explained, and there are
examples throughout to show you how to use the mathematics.

The book also includes:

- **Summaries** of the ideas met in each chapter, to help you
  study and revise.

- **Glossary** giving the meaning of mathematical words which
  you will meet in the course.

Your teacher will also give you **worksheets** during the course,
for practical work, homework or assessment.

# ontents

# 1  Networks

## A Nodes; regions; arcs

A **network** is a diagram of connected lines. Figure 1:1 is a network.

The points at which the lines meet are called **nodes**. There are three nodes in Figure 1:1. They are A, B and C.

Lines which join nodes are **arcs**. There are four arcs in Figure 1:1.

A space surrounded by arcs is a **region**. The space outside the network is also a region. There are three regions in Figure 1:1.

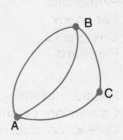

**Fig. 1:1**

### ● Some uses of networks

Town planners use networks when designing gas, electricity and water supplies, and when planning new traffic systems.

When roads are icy the routes of gritting lorries may be planned with the help of networks.

Sales representatives could use networks to make sure they travel to their customers by the shortest route.

Police computers reduce fingerprints to networks to make accurate comparisons between two prints.

Bus and underground train routes are often shown as networks, as are electrical and electronic circuits.

**A control network at a power station**

Do you use networks in any of your school subjects? Geography perhaps?

**1** Draw the networks in Figure 1:2.

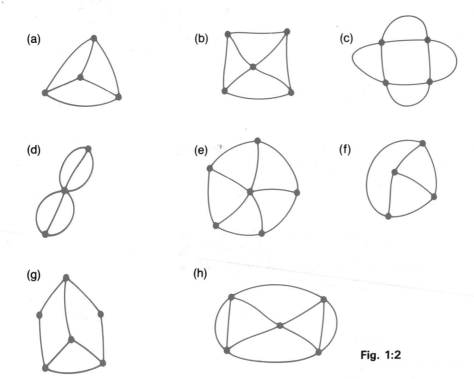

(a)  (b)  (c)  (d)  (e)  (f)  (g)  (h)

**Fig. 1:2**

Copy and complete this table for the networks.

| Network | Number of nodes (N) | Number of regions (R) | N + R | Number of arcs (A) |
|---------|---------------------|------------------------|-------|--------------------|
| (a)     |                     |                        |       |                    |
| (b)     |                     |                        |       |                    |
| (c)     |                     |                        |       |                    |
| etc.    |                     |                        |       |                    |

**2** Look at the table. Can you see a connection between the numbers in the last two columns? Write it down when you have found it.

**3** Draw some networks of your own. Do they all obey the rule you found in question 2?

Worksheet 1 may be used here.

# B Traversable networks

A network is **traversable** if it can be drawn without repeating a line or taking your pencil off the paper.

## ▶ Points to discuss . . .

Figure 1:3 shows a road map. A gritting lorry has to grit each road once, but not more than once. Figure 1:4 shows the map turned into a network, so that the quickest route can be planned.

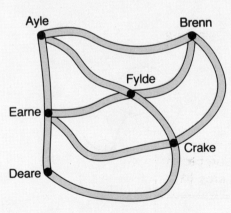

Fig. 1:3

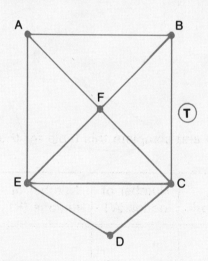

Fig. 1:4

1> Find a good route.

2> How many different routes are possible?

**1** Copy the networks in Figure 1:5. Write a large letter **T** beside those that are traversable.

(a)

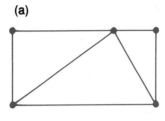

(b)

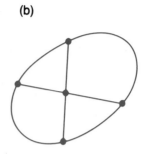

(c)

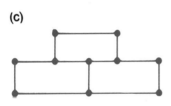

(d)

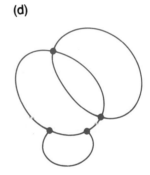

(e)

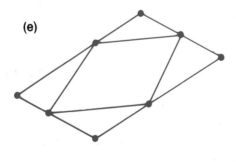

(f)

(g)

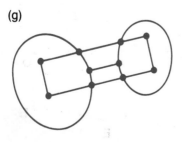

**Fig. 1:5**

**2** Which networks in Figure 1:6 are traversable?

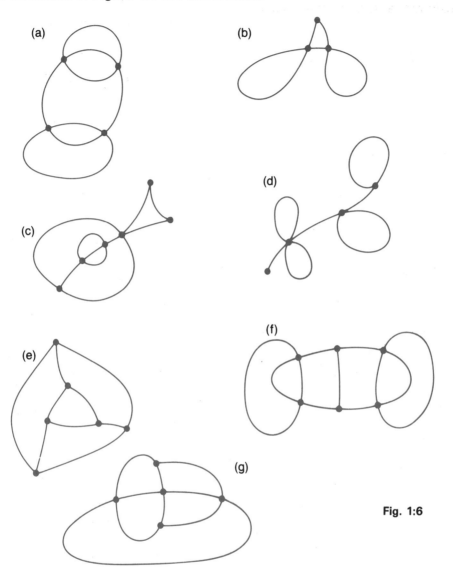

**Fig. 1:6**

**3** An **odd node** is one with an odd number of arcs leaving it. An **even node** is one with an even number of arcs leaving it.

**Example**   Figure 1:7 shows a network with the odd and even nodes marked.

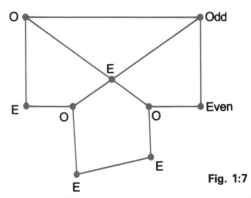

**Fig. 1:7**

Copy the networks in Figure 1:8 and mark the odd and even nodes.

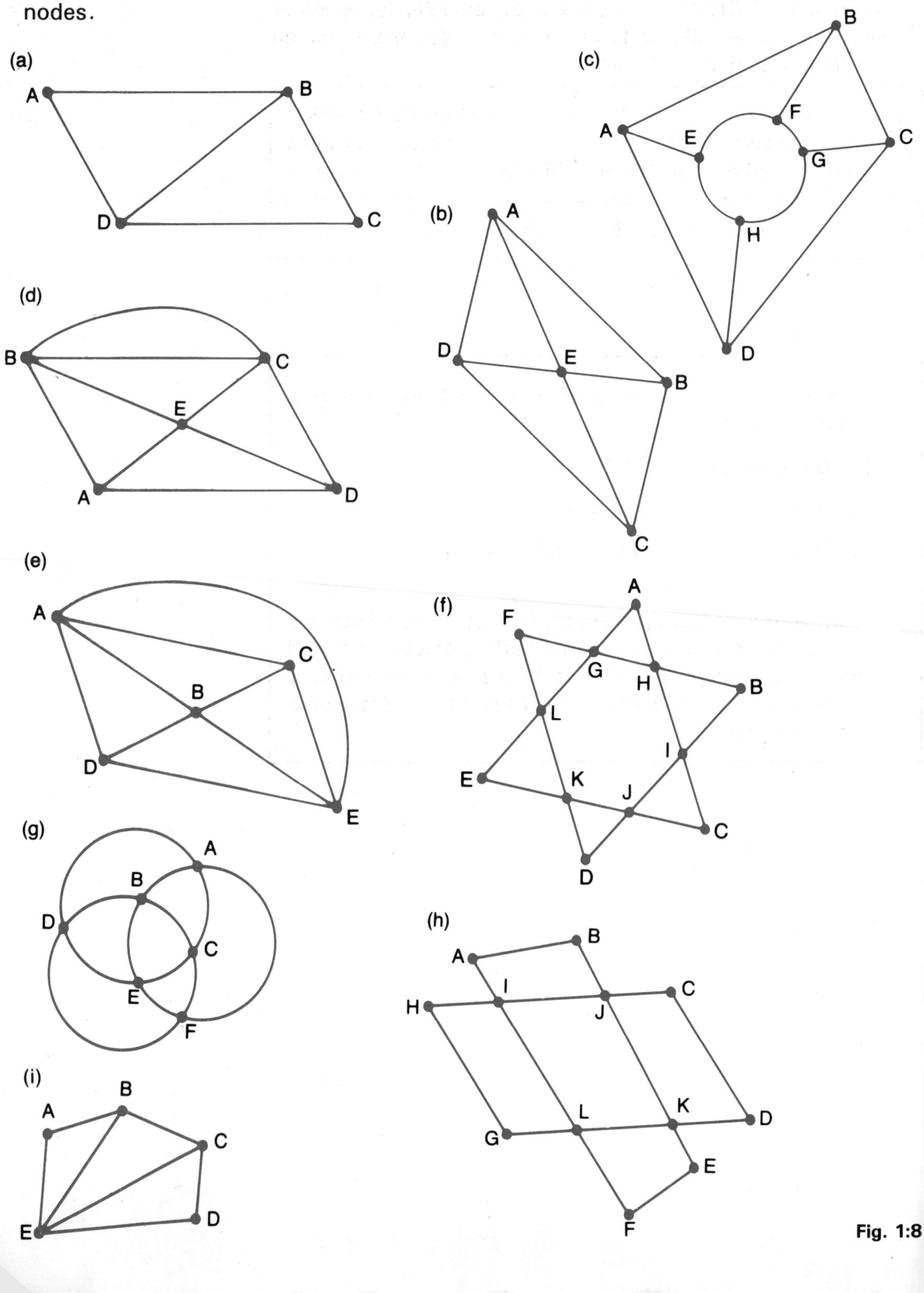

Fig. 1:8

4 Copy and complete this table for the networks you drew in question 3. Where the network is traversable, say whether you start at an odd node or an even node, and at which node(s) you start and finish.

| Network | Traversable? (Yes or No) | Start | Finish | Number of odd nodes | Number of even nodes |
|---|---|---|---|---|---|
| (a) | Yes; odd | B | D | 2 | 2 |
| etc. | | | | | |

5 Look at the table you made in question 4. What do you notice if:

(a) there are no odd nodes

(b) there are two odd nodes

(c) there are more than two odd nodes?

6 From your answers to question 5 write a rule which will tell you how to decide if a network is traversable, and where you should start if it is, by just considering how many odd and even nodes it has. Draw more networks to test your rule.

## A Columns

This **spike abacus** shows the **integer** (whole number) 1534.

We 'read' the number on the abacus from left to right:

There is one bead on the 1000s (thousands) spike.
There are five beads on the 100s (hundreds) spike.
There are three beads on the 10s (tens) spike.
There are four beads on the 1s (units) spike.

The number is **one thousand, five hundred and thirty-four.** (Thirty is short for 'three tens'.)

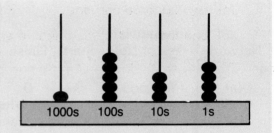

Fig. 2:1

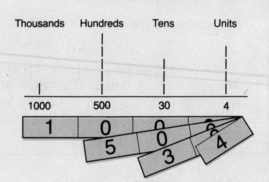

We could draw the spike abacus like this (Figure 2:2).

Fig. 2:2

1 Draw a picture like Figure 2:1 to show a spike abacus reading 1058.

2 Think how the number 4375 would look on the abacus. There is no need to draw it.

The 7 stands for 7 tens. What do these numbers stand for?

(a) The 3    (b) The 5    (c) The 4

3 What is the value of the 4 in each of these numbers?

(a) 421    (b) 1342    (c) 2054    (d) 4760

**4** **Example**   Twenty-seven in figures is 27.

Write these in figures.

(a)  forty-six       (b)  two hundred and ten

(c)  two hundred and one

(d)  one thousand, three hundred and eighty-seven

(e)  two thousand and one


**5**  When you write a cheque, you write the amount in words
as well as in figures. Write a sentence to explain why this
is done.

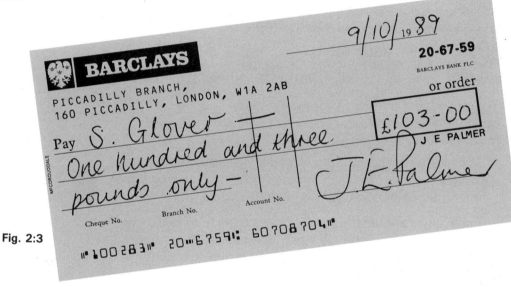

**Fig. 2:3**

Now write these in words.

(a)  24      (b)  113      (c)  209      (d)  42      (e)  1846

(f)  8020      (g)  1987      (h)  2014      (i)  2001


**6**  (a)  In which of the following does the 3 stand for 30?
        103      301      130      3000      1537

   (b)  In which of the following does the 4 stand for 400?
        574      457      4057      5438      6740

   (c)  In which of the following does the 5 stand for 5000?
        1125      5121      2511      1152      1537

   (d)  In which of the following does the 0 stand for no
        hundreds?
        1102      201      1021      3013      1210

Worksheet 2A may be used here.

7 Put the following lists of numbers in order of size, with the smallest first.

(a) 51, 15, 510, 150, 105, 501

(b) 213, 132, 321, 312, 231, 123

(c) 1243, 3241, 2431, 3412, 3421, 2341

8 Put the following lists of numbers in order of size, with the largest first.

(a) 70, 701, 170, 17, 107, 700

(b) 158, 815, 851, 518, 581, 185

(c) 1003, 3010, 1300, 3100, 3001, 1030

---

**9 A place value game for two players**

You will need 20 squares of paper or card, each about 2 cm square. Number your cards from 0 to 9 so that you have two cards with 0, two with 1, and so on.

Each player should draw a rectangle 8 cm long and 2 cm high. Divide the rectangle into four squares. They should be the same size as the squares you wrote the numbers on. Do not cut up your rectangles.

Shuffle the number cards and place them face down in a pile. The two players take turns to take the top card from the pile and place it on their rectangle.

The grid that shows the highest number when complete is the winner.

10 Look out for numbers in newspapers, books, magazines and posters. Make a collection of them. What is the largest number you can find? What is the smallest?

Look at each number and see if there is something special about it. For example, if you find the number 121 you might say that it is special because it is 11 × 11, or the square of 11. Also it is a palindromic number.

*Look this up in the glossary if you need to.*

A wall display of different numbers you see when travelling along a road would be fun to make. (Draw pictures of the numbers; do not pinch them!)

# B Addition and subtraction

Addition is putting the same kind of things together to find out how many there are altogether.

Subtraction is either taking away the same kind of things to find out how many are left, or finding the difference between two amounts, that is, how much bigger one is than the other.

## ▶ Points to discuss . . .

1 ▷ Another way of saying '2 add 3' is 'find the sum of 2 and 3'. How else could you say '2 add 3'?

2 ▷ Another way of saying '3 take away 1' is 'find the difference between 3 and 1'. How else could you say '3 take away 1'?

3 ▷ What examples of subtraction can be found in this picture?

Fig. 2:4

1  Write down the answer to:

   (a)  3 + 6      (b)  3 + 5 + 2      (c)  9 + 5

   (d)  8 + 5 + 1      (e)  8 + 3 + 2 + 1


2  Write down the answer to:

   (a)  1 + 3      (b)  1 + 3 + 5      (c)  1 + 3 + 5 + 7

   (d)  1 + 3 + 5 + 7 + 9


3  Did you notice a pattern in the parts of question 2? Did you
   notice anything special about the answers?

   What do you think part (e) would be? What is the answer?
   Does this fit your pattern?


4  Write down the answer to:

   (a)  9 − 5      (b)  8 − 3      (c)  11 − 3      (d)  19 − 4

   (e)  19 − 11


5  Write down the answer to:

   (a)  25 − 15      (b)  24 − 15      (c)  26 − 16

   (d)  26 − 17


6  Write down the answer to:

   (a)  52 − 32      (b)  52 − 33      (c)  67 − 27

   (d)  66 − 27


Worksheets 2B and 2C may be used here.


7  Make up some addition sums that you can do 'in your
   head'. Find the answers. You could check them with a
   calculator.

**8** Sally is finding the difference between 137 and 95.

What is the difference between:

(a)  11 and 3      (b)  14 and 21

(c)  59 and 27     (d)  15 and 67

(e)  123 and 99    (f)  123 and 89?

I need 5 to make 95 up to 100 then another 37 to make it 137. That's 37 plus 5, which is 42.

Worksheet 2D may be used here.

Fig. 2:5

**9** Make up some difference questions that you can do in your head. Find the answers. You could check your answers with a calculator.

By the way, can you check your answers without using the ⊟ key?

# C More about addition

When you cannot add numbers in your head you can use a written method. This is how Chang adds 24 and 218.

Fig. 2:6

Start with the units.
8 + 4 = 12
1 ten and 2 units.

$$\begin{array}{r} 24 \\ +\ 218 \\ \hline 2 \\ \end{array}$$
Carry

Now for the tens...

$$\begin{array}{r} 24 \\ +\ 218 \\ \hline 42 \\ \end{array}$$

$$\begin{array}{r} 24 \\ +\ 218 \\ \hline 242 \\ \end{array}$$

**1** Copy these and work out the answers.

(a)  56  
   + 25  
   ——

(b)  37  
   + 26  
   ——

(c)  24  
   + 18  
   ——

(d)  46  
   + 237  
   ——

(e)  159  
   + 22  
   ——

(f)  74  
   + 38  
   ——

(g)  186  
   + 45  
   ——

(h)  216  
   + 99  
   ——

(i)  138  
   + 203  
   ——

(j)  784  
   + 332  
   ——

(k)  888  
   + 666  
   ——

(l)  777  
   + 888  
   ——

(m)  999  
   + 999  
   ——

**2** How could you do question 1(m) in your head?

**3** Set these numbers out in columns, then add them to find the answers.

(a) 123 + 456      (b) 231 + 469

(c) 1238 + 276 + 22      (d) 1224 + 8775 + 346

(e) 5623 + 4328

**4** What is the sum of:

(a) 36 and 48      (b) 173 and 87      (c) 309 and 92?

**5** This table shows how many cars used a car park on each day during one week.

| Day | Monday | Tuesday | Wednesday | Thursday | Friday | Saturday | Sunday |
|-----|--------|---------|-----------|----------|--------|----------|--------|
| Cars | 395 | 604 | 608 | 391 | 582 | 417 | 103 |

How many cars used the car park during the week?

**6** Mrs Addmore collected the books used by pupils in the third year of her school. She recorded the numbers collected.

| Class | 3L | 3I | 3K | 3E | 3M | 3A | 3T | 3H | 3S |
|-------|----|----|----|----|----|----|----|----|----|
| Books | 29 | 28 | 27 | 30 | 26 | 25 | 29 | 27 | 28 |

How many books did she collect altogether?

---

**7** How many different additions can you make using some or all of the figures in the year you were born? You may use each figure once, twice, or not at all. What is the largest possible total?

---

# D More about subtraction

When we cannot do a subtraction in our heads, we can use a written method. Follow Nikita's method for 483 − 312.

$$
\begin{array}{r} 483 \\ -\,312 \\ \hline 1 \end{array}
\rightarrow
\begin{array}{r} 483 \\ -\,312 \\ \hline 71 \end{array}
\rightarrow
\begin{array}{r} 483 \\ -\,312 \\ \hline 171 \end{array}
$$

Start with the units. 3 take 2 leaves 1. Then do the tens and then the hundreds.

Fig. 2:7

Julie has a harder one to do. Follow her method.

Fig. 2:8

The units part is easy!

$$
\begin{array}{r} 325 \\ -132 \\ \hline 3 \end{array}
$$

I can't take 3 tens from 2 tens, so I move 1 hundred to the tens column. Then I have 2 hundreds and 12 tens.

**1** (a) 327    (b) 426    (c) 372    (d) 448
      − 118      − 207      − 213      − 219

**2** (a) 536    (b) 713    (c) 303    (d) 235
      − 245      − 231      − 112      − 144

**3** (a) 404    (b) 300    (c) 2041    (d) 1562
      − 125      − 136      − 1052      − 1373

**4** (a) 303 − 144     (b) 3124 − 1025     (c) 5210 − 25

**5** A travelling salesman copies his mileage counter every morning before he sets out on his work.

How many miles did the salesman travel:

(a) on Monday (work out 6255 − 6125)

(b) between Monday morning and Thursday morning

(c) on Wednesday

(d) on Tuesday, Wednesday and Thursday

(e) altogether that week if he travels 302 miles on Friday?

| | |
|---|---|
| Monday | 0 6 1 2 5 |
| Tuesday | 0 6 2 5 5 |
| Wednesday | 0 6 6 0 0 |
| Thursday | 0 6 7 9 4 |
| Friday | 0 7 0 0 0 |

Fig. 2:9

**6** Figure 2:10 shows the attendances at two football matches.

(a) What was the total attendance for both matches?

(b) How many more people went to last week's match than to this week's match?

Elwick
Football Club
**Attendance**
This week    3045
Last week    2876

Fig. 2:10

**7** (a) How many packets are left when 72 are taken from a full box of Crackers Crisps?

(b) If 36 are left in the box, how many have been taken out since it was full?

(c) How many packets will three full boxes contain?

Fig. 2:11

**8** In a school canteen, 183 fish fingers were served in the first sitting and 138 were served in the second sitting. The cook found that she had eight left over at the end of lunchtime.

(a) How many fish fingers were served altogether?

(b) How many fewer were served in the second sitting than in the first sitting?

(c) How many fish fingers were cooked altogether?

**9** A printer starts with one ream of paper, which is 500 sheets. After a print run, 275 sheets are printed on one side only and 80 are printed on both sides.

(a) How many more sheets are printed on one side than both sides?

(b) How many sheets of paper have not been printed at all?

Worksheet 2E may be used here.

**10** Write any three-figure number.
Now write it in reverse.
Find the difference between the two numbers.
Write the answer in reverse and add it to your answer.
What do you end up with?

Try this again with different starting numbers.

What happens if you start with a four-figure number?

Investigate further.

**11** Display 5078 on your calculator. Now find the *least* possible number of key presses, without pressing the cancel key, that will change 5078 into:

(a) 57    (b) 5278    (c) 5708    (d) 50 780
(e) 50 078

**12** Use an AA or similar book to find the number of people who live in the nearest town or city to your school. Use your own town or city if you wish.

(a)  Write this number and the name of the town or city.

(b)  Write the number in words.

(c)  Rearrange the digits to make the smallest number using all the digits.

(d)  Rearrange the digits to make the largest number using all the digits.

(e)  What do you notice about the answers to (c) and (d)? Investigate to find if this is true for other numbers and write briefly to say what you have found.

# 3  Calculators

When you use a calculator it is sensible to check your answer. Here are some ways that you can do this.

- **Think about the answer. Is it sensible?**

  **Example**  Hayley worked out that her family could have a fortnight's holiday on the Costa Del Sol at a total cost of £56·60. Is this sensible?

- **Do a rough estimate.**

  **Example**  $489 \times 52$ is roughly $500 \times 50$ which is 25 000. Marcel makes the answer 541. What did he do wrong?

- **Repeat the calculation.**

  This is not always a good check as you may make the same mistake again.

- **Use the answer to check your method.**

  This is a good check for simple arithmetic questions.

  **Example**  428 + 179  Answer 607
  Check by 607 − 179. (What should this come to?)

▶  ## Points to discuss . . .

How would you check these?

(a)  235 − 151 = 184      (b)  $312 \times 56 = 17\,472$

(c)  1000 ÷ 15 = 66·666 667

---

**1**  Check Anna's work in two ways. Briefly explain how you checked each one.

(a) 368 + 195 = 563        (b) 312 − 174 = 138

(c) 76 × 7 = 532            (d) 392 ÷ 8 = 49

**2** Check Tom's calculator exercise. If you find a wrong answer, copy the question and write the correct answer.

(a) $138 + 296 = 434$

(b) $421 - 138 = 263$

(c) $53 \times 18 = 459$

(d) $609 - 156 = 453$

(e) $416 \div 13 = 33$

(f) $297 + 538 = 835$

(g) $64 \times 37 = 1368$

(h) $1728 \div 12 = 166$

(i) $1001 - 365 = 636$

(j) $88 \times 88 = 4477$

**3** Majed had to calculate $238 + 121$, but he pressed the $\boxed{-}$ key instead of the $\boxed{+}$ key and so made the answer 117.

$\boxed{+}$, $\boxed{-}$, $\boxed{\times}$ and $\boxed{\div}$ are the operation keys.

In the following questions Majed sometimes pressed the wrong operation key. Find which questions he did wrongly, say which key he pressed by mistake, and write the correct answer.

(a) $249 + 135 = 114$

(b) $550 - 25 = 525$

(c) $47 \times 3 = 50$

(d) $265 - 130 = 395$

(e) $125 \div 5 = 625$

(f) $480 + 3 = 160$

(g) $75 + 25 = 3$

(h) $1000 - 11 = 1011$

(i) $275 - 190 = 85$

(j) $365 \times 15 = 380$

**4** (a) Find any two numbers which add to give the same answer as $179 + 165$.

(b) Find any two numbers which subtract to give the same answer as $308 - 169$.

**5** Getting the correct answer when the +, −, × or ÷ operation is given is straight forward. It becomes more difficult when you have to choose for yourself which operation key to press.

Example   Erica has to drive to Winchester, 120 miles away. It is now ten o'clock and she has to get there by one o'clock. What speed does she need to average?

She has to go 120 miles in 3 hours.
She must average 120 ★ 3 miles per hour.
What key is ★ ? $\boxed{+}$ , $\boxed{-}$ , $\boxed{×}$ , or $\boxed{÷}$ ?
Answer $\boxed{÷}$

Which key should be pressed in these questions?

(a) Tom is saving to buy a pair of trainers costing £15. He has saved £7 already. Tom needs £15 ★ £7 more.

(b) A class of 20 pupils visit a zoo. It costs 50p each to go in. Altogether the class has to pay 50 ★ 20 pence.

(c) Five friends go home from a disco by taxi. The taxi fare is £8. They share the cost equally. Each friend has to pay 8 ★ 5 pounds.

(d) Maria owes six friends 20p each. She needs 6 ★ 20 pence to pay them.

(e) Ranjit has 95p. He spends 18p. Ranjit has 95 ★ 18 pence left.

(f) A man saves half his earnings. He earns £185. He saves 185 ★ 2 pounds.

(g) Linda lives 48 km from Hinton. The distance to Hinton and back is 48 ★ 2 kilometres.

(h) There are 25 clips in a box. To buy 200 clips I need 200 ★ 25 boxes.

(i) A quarter of a class of 32 pupils cycle to school. The number who cycle is 32 ★ 4.

(j) Seventy-two boxes are arranged into 9 equal piles. Each pile contains 72 ★ 9 boxes.

**6** Work out the answers to question 5.

**7** In the following questions you may not be sure which key to press. Here are some ways to help you to decide.

- Try the same problem with smaller numbers.

- Try the problem with the key you think you should use. Now think carefully about your answer. Is it sensible?

(a) A church fund needs £18 000 to repair the steeple. So far the fund has raised £11 724. How much more is needed?

(b) It costs £3·50 to visit a county show. On Friday 8430 people paid to visit the show. How much money did the show organisers take on Friday?

(c) A youth club has 35 members. They decide to buy a snooker table costing £168. How much does each member of the youth club have to give?

(d) A shop overcharges 136 customers by 15p each. How much will the shop have to repay altogether?

(e) A jet aircraft takes off with 8560 kg of fuel and lands with 2790 kg of fuel. How much fuel was used?

(f) A quarter of a town of 13 660 people are pensioners. How many pensioners are there?

(g) The distance around a racetrack is 29 miles. How far will a car travel if it completes 115 laps of the track?

(h) There are 375 nails in a box. A carpenter needs 6000 nails. How many boxes are needed?

(i) Last week's attendance at a match was 11 742. This week the attendance increased by 3470. How many were there at the match this week?

(j) A lorry can carry 2450 bricks. How many lorries are needed to carry 78 400 bricks?

## 8 Adding consecutive numbers

(a) Use your calculator to find $1 + 2 + 3 + 4 + 5$. Now multiply the last number (5) by the middle number (3). What do you notice?

(b) Use your calculator to find
$1 + 2 + 3 + 4 + 5 + 6 + 7 + 8 + 9$.
Check your answer by adding it the other way $(9 + 8 + \ldots)$. Now multiply the last number by the middle number. What do you notice?

(c) Find $1 + 2 + 3 + 4 + \ldots + 17 + 18 + 19$.

> *HINT!*
> *The middle number is 10.*

(d) Find a simple rule to work out what the middle number is.

(e) Add all the whole numbers from 1 to 37.

(f) Add all the whole numbers from 1 to 51.

(g) Add all the whole numbers from 1 to 99.

(h) Add all the whole numbers from 1 to 979.

(i) Can you find a quick way to add all the numbers from 1 to 1000? If you find this difficult, try it with all the numbers from 1 to 10.

## 9 Palindromic numbers

A palindromic number is one which reads the name forwards as backwards, like 32523.

| Example | Take any number | 168 | |
|---|---|---|---|
| | Reverse the digits | 861 | Step one |
| | Add | 1029 | |
| | Reverse the digits | 9201 | Step two |
| | Add | 10230 | |
| | Reverse the digits | 03201 | Step three |
| | Add | 13431 | A palindrome! |

168 became a palindromic number in three steps.

Use your calculator to find how many steps are needed to make a palindromic number from:

(a) 39    (b) 49    (c) 68    (d) 69    (e) 79

Investigate numbers of your own.

# A Turning

## ▶ Points to discuss . . .

1 > Do doors turn? What about a pendulum? Make a list, draw or collect pictures of things which turn.

2 > Figure 4:1 shows how the hands of a clock turn during 1 hour.

Fig. 4:1

The minute hand is the longer one. How long does it take to make a complete turn?

The hour hand is the shorter one. How long does it take to make a complete turn?

3 > Look at Figure 4:2.

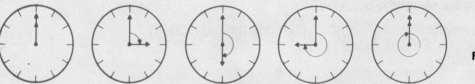

Fig. 4:2

- The first clock shows 12 o'clock.

- The second clock shows the time three hours later. It is 3 o'clock. The hour hand has turned a quarter turn.

- The third clock shows the time after another three hours. Now it is 6 o'clock. The hour hand has turned a half turn altogether.

- At 9 o'clock the hour hand has made three-quarters of a turn.

- When the hour hand has made a complete turn it is 12 o'clock again.

The way a clock hand turns is called **clockwise**.
The opposite way is called **anti-clockwise**.

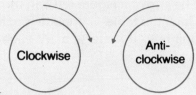

Fig. 4:3

1  The arrow in Figure 4:4 can turn to point at different letters. Copy the table. Complete it to show which letter the arrow points to if it starts at A each time and turns clockwise.

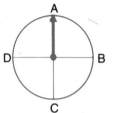

Fig. 4:4

|   | After turning clockwise from A | The arrow will point to |
|---|---|---|
| (a) | a half turn | C |
| (b) | a quarter turn | |
| (c) | a whole turn | |
| (d) | a three-quarter turn | |
| (e) | one and a half turns | |
| (f) | one and a quarter turns | |

2  What would the answers to question 1 have been if the arrow had turned anti-clockwise?

3  Look again at Figure 4:4. Copy and complete the table for quarter turns.

| It is a quarter turn from | to |
|---|---|
| B | A |
| B | C |
| C | |
| C | |
| D | |
| D | |
| A | |
| A | |

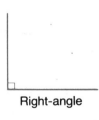

Right-angle

Fig. 4:5

This is the sign for a right-angle. A right-angle is a quarter turn.

**4** The arrow in Figure 4:6 can turn to point at different letters. Copy the table. Complete it to show which letter the arrow points to if it starts at W each time and turns clockwise.

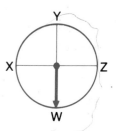

Fig. 4:6

|  | Clockwise from W | Points to |
|---|---|---|
| (a) | $1\frac{1}{2}$ turns | Y |
| (b) | 1 turn | |
| (c) | $\frac{1}{4}$ turn | |
| (d) | $\frac{3}{4}$ turn | |
| (e) | $1\frac{1}{4}$ turns | |
| (f) | $1\frac{3}{4}$ turns | |

**5** What would the answers to question 4 be if the arrow had turned anti-clockwise?

**6** Look at Figure 4:6. Answer 'Yes' or 'No' to say whether each of the following turns are right-angle turns or not. In each case the arrow turns the shortest way from the first letter to the second.

(a) W to Z    (b) W to X    (c) X to Y    (d) X to Z

(e) Y to Z    (f) X to W    (g) W to Y

**7** In Figure 4:7 the lines drawn from 12 and 3 to the centre make a right-angle.

Copy and complete the table to show other pairs of numbers that make a right-angle when joined to the centre.

Fig. 4:7

| First number | 3 | 3 | 5 | 5 | 8 | 8 | 10 | 10 | 1 | 1 | 12 | 12 | 6 | 6 |
|---|---|---|---|---|---|---|---|---|---|---|---|---|---|---|
| Second number | | | | | | | | | | | | | | |

8 Copy and complete the table to say how many turns are made by the minute hand (the longer one) on a clock between the given times.

|     | From | To | The minute hand makes |
|-----|------|----|-----------------------|
| (a) | 9 o'clock | 10 o'clock | 1 turn |
| (b) | 8 o'clock | 11 o'clock | |
| (c) | 7 o'clock | half past 7 | |
| (d) | half past 2 | half past 3 | |
| (e) | half past 3 | 5 o'clock | |
| (f) | 9 o'clock | quarter past 9 | |
| (g) | quarter past 8 | quarter to 9 | |
| (h) | quarter past 7 | half past 8 | |
| (i) | quarter to 2 | quarter to 5 | |
| (j) | half past one | quarter to 12 | |

9 What is the time if the minute hand turns as in the table?

|     | Number of turns | Starting time |
|-----|-----------------|---------------|
| (a) | 1 | 8 o'clock |
| (b) | $\frac{1}{2}$ | 1 o'clock |
| (c) | $\frac{3}{4}$ | 2 o'clock |
| (d) | $1\frac{1}{2}$ | half past 3 |
| (e) | $2\frac{1}{2}$ | half past 5 |
| (f) | $1\frac{3}{4}$ | quarter to eight |

10 Make a list of everyday things which turn through an angle. Estimate the size of the angle as a number of turns.

11 Find out about patterns that can be made by turning shapes.

# B Using a protractor

We usually measure the amount of turn in **degrees**. A complete turn is 360 degrees. The sign for degrees is °.

We use a ruler to measure length in centimetres. We use a **protractor** to measure a turn, or an angle, in degrees.

*Try to find out why 360 is used.*

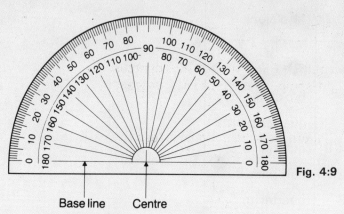

Base line    Centre

Fig. 4:9

Whole turn
360 degrees
360°

Half turn
180 degrees
180°

Quarter turn
90 degrees
90°

Three-quarters turn
270 degrees
270°

Fig. 4:8

Look at Figure 4:9. Compare it with your protractor. Notice how the numbers are repeated, one lot going from left to right (clockwise), the others going anti-clockwise. **You have to be careful to use the correct number.**

When you have measured lots of angles you will be able to guess how many degrees an angle is. This is a good way to check that you have read the correct number.

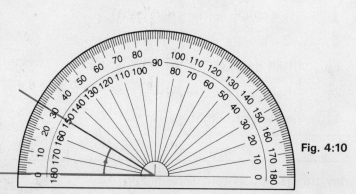

Fig. 4:10

In Figure 4:10 you could read the answer as 30 degrees or 150 degrees, but as the turn is less than a right-angle it must be 30 degrees.

*How many degrees is a right-angle?*

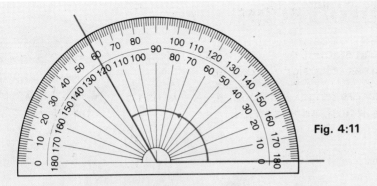

**Fig. 4:11**

In Figure 4:11 the answer could be 60 degrees or 120 degrees.
The turn is more than a right-angle, so it must be 120 degrees.

**1** Measure each angle in Figure 4:12. Each angle is less than
a right-angle.

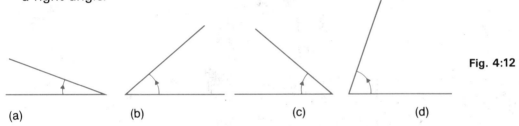

**Fig. 4:12**

(a)          (b)          (c)          (d)

**2** Measure each angle in Figure 4:13. Each angle is less than
90 degrees.

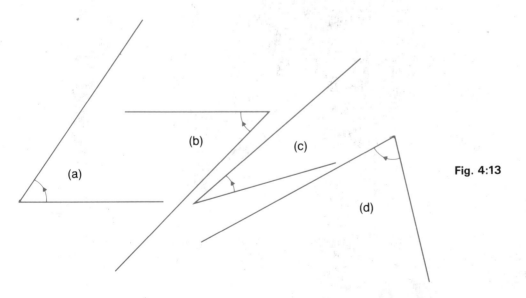

(b)

(c)

(a)

**Fig. 4:13**

(d)

**3** Measure each angle in Figure 4:14.

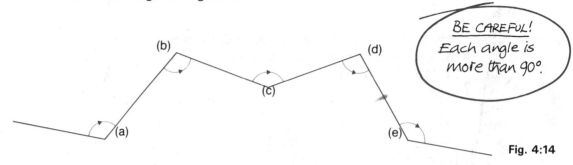

BE CAREFUL!
Each angle is
more than 90°.

Fig. 4:14

**4** Measure the angles in Figure 4:15.

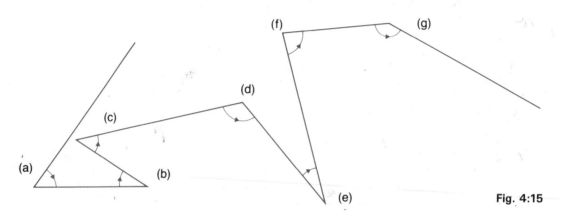

Fig. 4:15

Worksheet 4A may be used here.

**5** (a) Look at Figure 4:16. It shows a compass. What do N, E, S and W stand for?

(b) You could make a compass like Figure 4:16 by folding a circle of paper.

(c) NE stands for north-east. It is 45° from north to north-east.
SW stands for south-west. It is 225° from north to south-west. We always measure from north in a clockwise direction.
Copy Figure 4:16, or use the paper circle compass in part (b). Use your calculator to find out how many degrees should be written in the empty boxes.

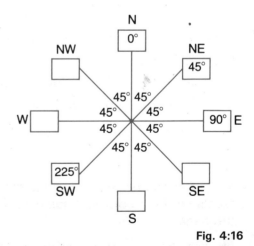

Fig. 4:16

Worksheets 4B and 4C may be used here.

**6** John faces north, then makes a clockwise turn. Copy and complete the table to show the direction in which he then faces. Each turn starts from north.

|     | Clockwise turn from north | John now faces |
| --- | --- | --- |
| (a) | 180° | S |
| (b) | 90° | |
| (c) | 135° | |
| (d) | 270° | |
| (e) | 225° | |
| (f) | 315° | |
| (g) | 45° | |
| (h) | 360° | |

**7** What is the size of the smaller angle between the hands of a clock at:

(a) 1 o'clock     (b) 4 o'clock     (c) 6 o'clock

(d) 9 o'clock     (e) 11 o'clock     (f) 3 o'clock

(g) 5 o'clock     (h) 7 o'clock     (i) 10 o'clock?

**8** A fly is sitting on the end of the minute hand of a clock face on a church tower. A spider is sitting half-way along the hand.

(a) Which travels further in an hour, the spider or the fly?

(b) Which travels faster?

# C Kinds of angle

Figure 4:17 shows how to make an angle maker.

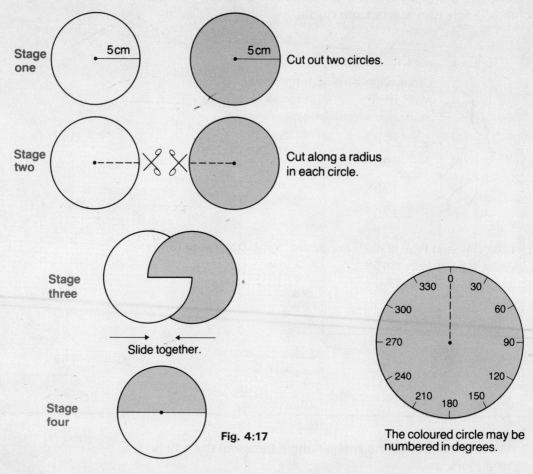

Stage one — 5cm — 5cm — Cut out two circles.

Stage two — Cut along a radius in each circle.

Stage three — Slide together.

Stage four

Fig. 4:17

The coloured circle may be numbered in degrees.

Figure 4:18 shows an angle maker set to each of the four special kinds of angle.

Fig. 4:18

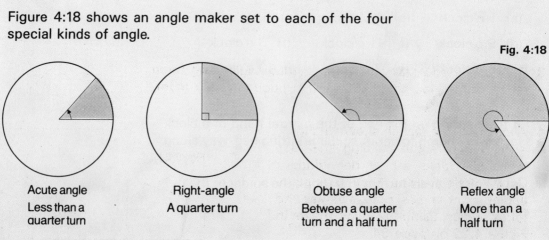

Acute angle
Less than a quarter turn

Right-angle
A quarter turn

Obtuse angle
Between a quarter turn and a half turn

Reflex angle
More than a half turn

**1** Look at the angles in Figure 4:19. Some of them are acute and some are obtuse. Write the correct name for each angle.

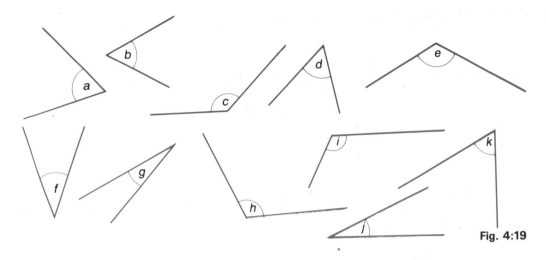

Fig. 4:19

**2** The angles in Figure 4:20 are acute, right, obtuse or reflex. Write the correct name for each angle.

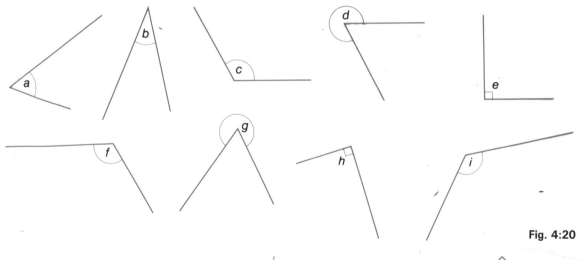

Fig. 4:20

**3** Draw three acute angles, three obtuse angles and three reflex angles. You could ask another pupil to check them.

**4** Alice made the sketch shown in Figure 4:21. It shows the building she sees when she looks out of her window. Copy Alice's drawing, then mark acute angles, right-angles, obtuse angles and reflex angles, using the signs shown in Figure 4:22 on page 34.

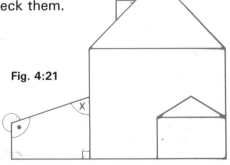

Fig. 4:21

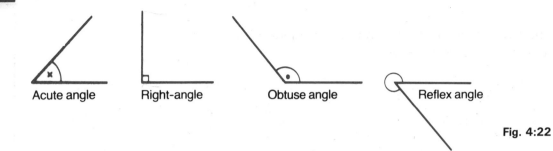

Acute angle      Right-angle      Obtuse angle      Reflex angle

Fig. 4:22

**5** Copy and complete the table.

| Turn | Degrees |
|------|---------|
| Quarter turn | 90° |
| Half turn | |
| Whole turn | |
| Three-quarter turn | |

**6** Copy and complete this table. All turns are clockwise from the first compass point to the second. Figure 4:16 will help you.

| | Turning clockwise from | Turning clockwise to | Number of degrees turned | Kind of angle |
|------|------|------|------|------|
| (a) | N | NE | 45° | Acute |
| (b) | E | SE | | |
| (c) | W | NW | | |
| (d) | NW | E | | |
| (e) | SW | N | | |
| (f) | E | NE | | |
| (g) | SW | SE | | |
| (h) | NE | SE | | |

**7** Fold two pieces of paper as shown in Figure 4:23. What two angles do you make?

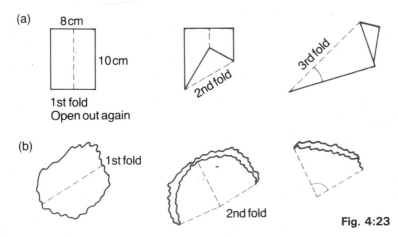

(a)

1st fold
Open out again

2nd fold

3rd fold

(b)

1st fold

2nd fold

Fig. 4:23

Can you make 60° with (a) and 45° with (b)?

Investigate other folded angles.

**8** Draw a picture of some buildings, either real ones seen from your window, or imaginary ones. Mark the different kinds of angles in your picture, as shown in Figure 4:22.

# D Drawing angles

Figure 4:24 shows how to draw an angle of 30°.

Angle required

Step one

Step two

Step three

Fig. 4:24

**Remember**

- Line up your protractor's base line with the drawn line (MA).

- Have the centre of the protractor exactly at the point where you want the angle (M).

- Use the correct set of numbers (the inside 30 in Figure 4:9).

**1** Use a protractor to draw the angles shown in Figure 4:25.

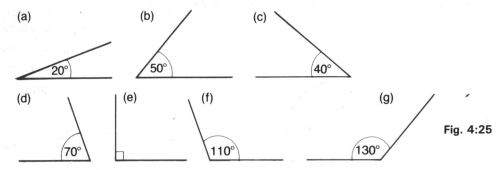

Fig. 4:25

**2** Draw a line of length 4 cm. At the left-hand end of the line draw an angle of 55°. At the right-hand end of the line draw an angle of 35°. Have you drawn a triangle? If not, make your angle lines longer until you have. Measure the third angle in the triangle.

**3** Figure 4:26 shows a designer's specifications for some letters to be used on a poster. Draw the letters full size to the measurements given by the designer.

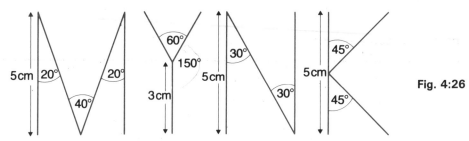

Fig. 4:26

**4** Copy the diagrams in Figure 4:27 to the sizes given.

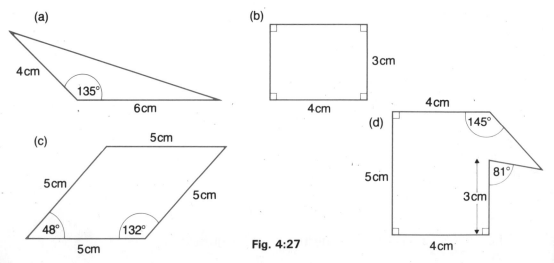

Fig. 4:27

**5** Figure 4:28 shows you how to draw a circle using a 180°
protractor.

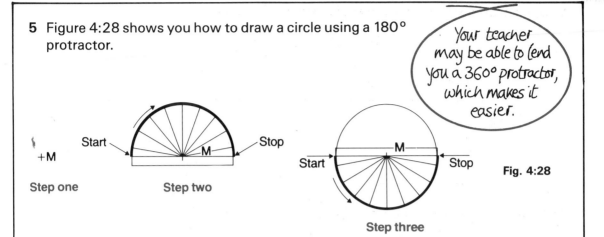

*Your teacher may be able to lend you a 360° protractor, which makes it easier.*

**Step one**  **Step two**  **Step three**

**Fig. 4:28**

Draw a circle round a protractor.

Mark every 10° as accurately as you can, marking
outside the circle. Now use a ruler and a fine-point pen
or a sharp pencil to join every point marked on the circle
to every other point. The resulting pattern is called a
Mystic Rose.

**6** Design some patterns of your own.

# Decimals: addition and subtraction

## A Tenths and hundredths

▶ **Points to discuss . . .**

| 1000s | 100s | 10s | 1s |
|-------|------|-----|----|

1. ▷ If we continue the columns to the left, what will the next column be?

2. ▷ If we continue the columns to the right, what will the next column be?

3. ▷ How many more columns going to the right can you name? What are their names?

Look at Figure 5:1. It shows the number 'four hundred and twenty-one point three five'.

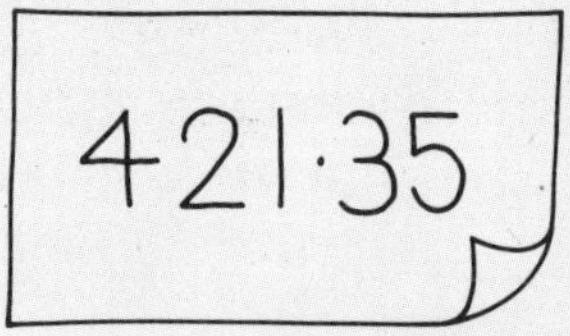

$$421 \cdot 35$$

The point is called the **decimal point**. It shows where the whole numbers end and the fractions begin.

**Fig. 5:1**

Note that we should not say 'point thirty-five', although we break this rule with money. When do we do this?

Figure 5:2 is a rectangle divided into 10 squares.

**Fig. 5:2**

In Figure 5:3 three of the squares have been shaded. This is **three tenths** of the rectangle, or **0·3** of the rectangle.
0·7 of the rectangle is not shaded.
0·3 + 0·7 together make a whole one.

**Fig. 5:3**

**1** The first column after the decimal point is a column of tenths. What is the second column after the decimal point?

**2** Write, like 0·3 and 0·7, the amount shaded and not shaded in the rectangles in Figure 5:4.

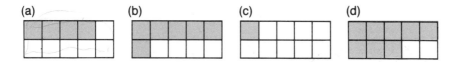

(a)        (b)        (c)        (d)

Fig. 5:4

**3** In Figure 5:5, 0·8 (eight tenths) and 0·5 (five tenths) of two rectangles have been added together to make thirteen tenths, or one whole rectangle and three tenths.
We can write this as

$$0·8 + 0·5 = 1·3 \text{ (one point three)}.$$

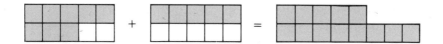

Fig. 5:5

(a) Look at Figure 5:6.
Write as a decimal fraction, like 0·3 and 1·3, the amount shaded in:
(i) A    (ii) B   (iii) C   (iv) D   (v) E
(vi) F   (vii) G   (viii) H

(b) Write as a decimal the amount shaded in:
(i) A + B    (ii) B + C   (iii) C + D   (iv) E + F
(v) F + G   (vi) G + H   (vii) A + B + C
(viii) B + E + G  (ix) F + G + H
(x) B + D + F

(c) A + F makes 1 whole. Which others make 1 whole?

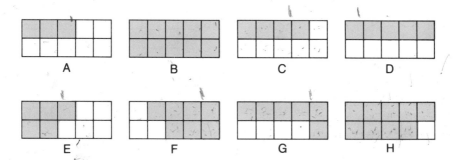

A        B        C        D

E        F        G        H

Fig. 5:6

4 Write in figures, using a decimal point:

   (a) 5 units and 3 tenths    (b) 2 units and 9 tenths

   (c) no units and 2 tenths    (d) 7 tenths

   (e) 10 units and 5 tenths

5 Write in figures:

   (a) nine point six    (b) eleven point four

   (c) twenty-seven point eight    (d) fifty point three

   (e) two hundred and fifteen point one

6 **Example** 13·7 is 1 ten, 3 units, 7 tenths.

   Write in a similar way:

   (a) 15·2   (b) 7·1   (c) 30·3   (d) 156·4

7 Figure 5:7 shows a square. Count the small squares. *100*

Each small square is one hundredth or 0·01 of the large square.

If you shade 4 small squares (A) you have shaded 0·04 or 4 hundredths of the large square.
If you shade 10 small squares (B) you have shaded 0·10 or 10 hundredths of the large square.
Altogether 14 small squares are shaded; that is 0·14 of the large square.

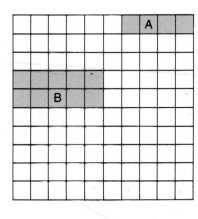

Fig. 5:7

  (a) How many small squares are there in Figure 5:8?

  (b) Write as a decimal fraction of the large square (like 0·4 and 0·14):
     (i) C    (ii) D    (iii) E
     (iv) F    (v) G    (vi) C + D
     (vii) D + E    (viii) F + G

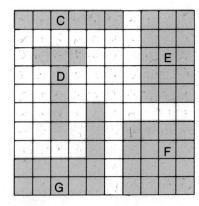

Fig. 5:8

8 What decimal fraction of Figure 5:8 is not shaded?

**9** Figure 5:9 shows 1 whole square shaded, together with 8 hundredths and 24 hundredths of another square.

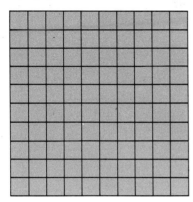 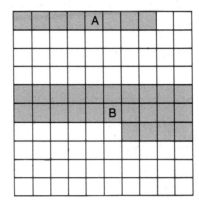

Fig. 5:9

Altogether 1 + 0·08 + 0·24 = 1·32 is shaded.
1·32 is 1 whole square and 32 hundredths, or 132 hundredths altogether.

Write as a decimal:

(a) 1 hundredth (b) 9 hundredths

(c) 27 hundredths (d) 3 hundredths

(e) 20 hundredths (f) 40 hundredths

**10 Example** 35·07 is read 'thirty-five point nought seven' or 'thirty-five point zero seven'.

Write in words:

(a) 16·05 (b) 82·17 (c) 16·39 (d) 40·14

(e) 40·01

**11** Write in figures:

(a) twenty-four point nought six

(b) thirty point one nine

(c) fifty point zero two seven

(d) one hundred and twenty point three five

(e) ten point nought one

**12** What is the value of the figure 3 in:

(a) 35 (b) 93 (c) 1·3 (d) 2·53 (e) 0·3?

**13** Copy and complete this table:

| Hundreds | | | | | thousandths |
|---|---|---|---|---|---|
| 100s | | | • | | 0·001s |

**14** **Example** 124·506 is read 'one hundred and twenty-four point five zero six'.

Write in words:

(a) 152·075    (b) 2·001    (c) 15·17    (d) 160·205

**15** **Example** 57·602 is 5 tens, 7 units, 6 tenths, no hundredths, 2 thousandths.

Write in a similar way:

(a) 64·305    (b) 156·028    (c) 100·235

**16** What is the value of the figure 5 in:

(a) 521·136    (b) 27·582    (c) 1·058    (d) 7·025?

**17** Say which is the larger.

(a) 0·3 or 0·9    (b) 6·8 or 7    (c) 6 or 0·6

(d) 1·4 or 4·4    (e) 2·1 or 2·0

**18** Draw a line of length:

(a) 10 cm    (b) 1 cm    (c) 3·5 cm    (d) 0·7 cm

(e) 10·1 cm

**19** What are the readings on the scales in Figure 5:10?    (c)

(a)

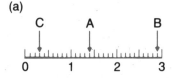

(b)

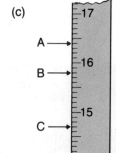

**20** Find out about other scales.

Fig. 5:10

# B Addition and subtraction

When adding or subtracting decimal numbers without a calculator you must line up the units column. This puts the decimal points in line too, but you may have whole numbers with no decimal point.

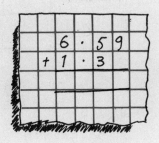

**1** (a)    4·5
      + 1·3
      ‾‾‾‾‾

     (b)    23·4
      +  4·2
      ‾‾‾‾‾

     (c)    5·3
      + 32·4
      ‾‾‾‾‾

     (d)    27·6
      + 31·2
      ‾‾‾‾‾

     (e)    124·5
      +   5·2
      ‾‾‾‾‾

**2** (a)    3·9
      + 1·5
      ‾‾‾‾‾

     (b)    7·6
      + 11·7
      ‾‾‾‾‾

     (c)    24·8
      +  7·4
      ‾‾‾‾‾

     (d)    16·7
      + 39·6
      ‾‾‾‾‾

     (e)    7·8
      + 8·7
      ‾‾‾‾‾

**3** (a)    5·62
      + 1·35
      ‾‾‾‾‾

     (b)    4·74
      + 13·15
      ‾‾‾‾‾

     (c)    6·59
      + 1·3
      ‾‾‾‾‾

     (d)    8·75
      + 7·19
      ‾‾‾‾‾

     (e)    0·86
      + 4·75
      ‾‾‾‾‾

**4** (a)    8·7
      − 1·5
      ‾‾‾‾‾

     (b)    3·95
      − 1·24
      ‾‾‾‾‾

     (c)    29·05
      − 13·01
      ‾‾‾‾‾

     (d)    4·61
      − 1·4
      ‾‾‾‾‾

     (e)    14·85
      −  3·02
      ‾‾‾‾‾

**5** (a) $\begin{array}{r} 5\cdot4 \\ -\ 1\cdot8 \\ \hline \end{array}$ (b) $\begin{array}{r} 6\cdot25 \\ -\ 1\cdot17 \\ \hline \end{array}$ (c) $\begin{array}{r} 18\cdot55 \\ -\ 7\cdot48 \\ \hline \end{array}$

(d) $\begin{array}{r} 9\cdot14 \\ -\ 7\cdot36 \\ \hline \end{array}$ (e) $\begin{array}{r} 5\cdot48 \\ -\ 4\cdot59 \\ \hline \end{array}$

**6** (a) $7\cdot6 + 8\cdot9$ (b) $8\cdot3 - 4\cdot2$ (c) $18\cdot7 - 6\cdot9$

(d) $20\cdot5 - 1\cdot9$ (e) $5\cdot1 - 0\cdot8$

**7** When whole numbers are included, be careful to line up the units figures. You can write in zeros to make up the empty columns if you like. You **must** put in zeros when you are taking away from a whole number.

**Examples** (a) $3\cdot75 + 8$
$$\begin{array}{r} 3\cdot75 \\ +\ 8 \\ \hline 11\cdot75 \end{array} \quad \text{or} \quad \begin{array}{r} 3\cdot75 \\ +\ 8\cdot00 \\ \hline 11\cdot75 \end{array}$$

(b) $5 - 1\cdot23$
$$\begin{array}{r} 5\cdot00 \\ -\ 1\cdot23 \\ \hline 3\cdot77 \end{array}$$

(a) $7 + 4\cdot9$ (b) $7 - 4\cdot9$ (c) $15 + 0\cdot85$
(d) $12 - 1\cdot5$ (e) $14\cdot25 - 9$

**8** (a) $4\cdot65 + 5 + 1\cdot9$ (b) $18\cdot7 + 15\cdot9 + 4$

(c) $6\cdot05 + 0\cdot8 + 8$

**9** (a) What is the sum of $4\cdot35$ and 7?

(b) What is the difference between $6\cdot1$ and $1\cdot25$?

(c) From $10\cdot2$ take $1\cdot4$.

(d) Take $0\cdot7$ from 2.

(e) What must be added to $1\cdot8$ to make 3?

**10** (a) $10 - 1\cdot8$ (b) $10 - 0\cdot4$ (c) $10 - 1\cdot25$

(d) $10 - 0\cdot01$ (e) $10 - 1\cdot01$

**11** (a) Add $3 \cdot 64$ to $1 \cdot 36$ on paper.

(b) Add $3 \cdot 64$ and $1 \cdot 36$ with your calculator.

(c) Write about your answers. Are they the same? Should they be the same?

(d) Check your answers to questions 1 to 10 with a calculator.

---

**12** Copy and complete these tables. Say for each table by how much the **total** of all the changed numbers would increase or decrease.

(a)

| Number | Increase the tenths column by 1 |
|---|---|
| $7 \cdot 48$ | |
| $0 \cdot 2$ | |
| $0 \cdot 39$ | |
| $8 \cdot 9$ | |
| $0 \cdot 99$ | |

(b)

| Number | Increase the hundredths column by 1 |
|---|---|
| $6 \cdot 25$ | |
| $0 \cdot 4$ | |
| $0 \cdot 19$ | |
| $7 \cdot 9$ | |
| $0 \cdot 99$ | |

(c)

| Number | Decrease the tenths column by 1 |
|---|---|
| $6 \cdot 35$ | |
| $0 \cdot 5$ | |
| $0 \cdot 15$ | |
| $7 \cdot 0$ | |
| $6 \cdot 05$ | |

(d)

| Number | Decrease the hundredths column by 1 |
|---|---|
| $5 \cdot 75$ | |
| $0 \cdot 12$ | |
| $0 \cdot 3$ | |
| $4 \cdot 0$ | |
| $6 \cdot 1$ | |

# C Money: addition and subtraction

Ten 10p coins = 100p or £1

$10p = \frac{1}{10}$ of £1 = £0·10

One hundred 1p coins = 100p or £1

$1p = \frac{1}{100}$ of £1 = £0·01

Fig. 5:11

1  Look at the following amounts of money. Rewrite correctly
   any that you think are written wrongly.

   (a) £5     (b) 8£     (c) £0·30     (d) £0·7

   (e) £44p     (f) 17p     (g) £1.65     (h) 235p

   (i) £4·0     (j) £·28     (k) £6·15p

2  How many pence make:

   (a) £1     (b) £3     (c) £0·65     (d) £1·78?

3  Write in pounds:

   (a) 325p     (b) 78p     (c) 9p     (d) 1250p

4  John bought the items shown in Figure 5:12 before starting
   at his new school. How much did he pay altogether?

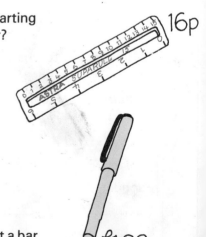

16p

Fig. 5:12

£5·15

5  What change would you receive from £1 if you bought a bar
   of chocolate costing 48p?

£1·28

**6** Look at Figure 5:13.

  (a) Which two items come to exactly £1?

  (b) What is the total cost of all four items?

  (c) What change will you receive from £5 if you buy all four items?

**Fig. 5:13**

**7** By how much has the radio in Figure 5:14 been reduced in the sale?

**Fig. 5:14**

**8** What is the sale price of the toaster in Figure 5:15?

**Fig. 5:15**

**9** Find the missing amounts in this table.

| Item | Usual price | Sale price | Reduced by |
|---|---|---|---|
| Football | £7·35 | £5·80 | |
| Shorts | £3·20 | | £0·95 |
| Racquet | £14·50 | | £5·65 |
| Trainers | £9·15 | £7·68 | |
| Sports bag | | £8·45 | £3·85 |

**10 Example**    £4·34 + 95p + £7 + 8p

```
    £
    4·34
    0·95
    7·00
    0·08
   12·37
```

Write the following amounts in columns, then add them.

(a)  £2·33,  £1·49,  £12      (b)  £7·99,  £0·45,  25p

(c)  £4,  £2·16,  36p      (d)  £18·90,  £0·95,  £9,  90p

(e)  £14,  3p,  18p,  £3·62,  6p

**11** Work these out. Check your answers by addition.

(a)  £6·24 − £4·36      (b)  £11·16 − £7·09

(c)  £5·00 − £3·27      (d)  £10 − £1·43

(e)  £5 − £4·37      (f)  £20 − £13·09

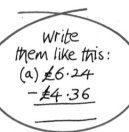

write them like this:

(a) £6.24
   −£4.36

**12** Some pupils made a mistake in each of the following. Find out what they did wrong, then work out the correct answers.

(a)  £6·25 + £5

```
   6·25
 +    5    ✗
 £6·30
```

(b)  £7·28 + £16

```
   7·28
 +   16    ✗
 £7·44
```

(c)  £5·43 + £8·29

```
   5·43
 + 8·29    ✗
 £13·81
```

(d)  £6·32 − £4·88

```
 £4·88
 £6·32
 £2·56    ✗
```

(e)  £4 − £3·26

```
 £4·00
 3·26
 1·26    ✗
```

(f)  £3·62 + £8 + 3p

```
 £3·62
     8
     3
 £4·00    ✗
```

**13** Evita used a calculator to add £2·24 and 87p. She gave the answer as £89·24. Can this be correct? What do you think she did? What should she have done?

14 Use a calculator to find the answers to the following. In each case think whether your answer is sensible.

(a) £5·36 + 85p     (b) £4 − £0·80

(c) £5 − £1·08     (d) £10 − 64p

(e) £2·50 + £30 + 65p     (f) £1·70 + 68p + 7p

(g) 89p + 4p + 82p + 9p + 6p     (h) £5 − 9p

(i) £1 − 8p

15 Work out the answers to the following questions in your head.

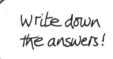

*Write down the answers!*

(a) What is the change from £1 when you spend:
    (i) 95p     (ii) 82p     (iii) 57p     (iv) 26p     (v) 18p?

(b) What is the change from £5 when you spend:
    (i) £4·80     (ii) £3·80     (iii) £2·40
    (iv) £1·36     (v) £2·13?

16 I give a shopkeeper £10 to pay for groceries costing £3·38. When he gives me the change he says, '40, 50, £4, £5, £10'. What coins or notes does he give me? Is my change correct?

17 What coins or notes were given in the following examples?

(a) Groceries cost £2·79. The grocer says, '80, £3, £4, £5, £10.'

(b) Groceries cost £8·23. The grocer says, '25, 30, 50, £9, £10.'

(c) Groceries cost £9·83. The grocer says, '84, 85, 95, £10.'

18 For each of the following the grocer gives you as few coins and notes as possible. She always gives the change in order from least value to greatest value as in question 17. What would she say?

| | (a) | (b) | (c) | (d) | (e) | (f) | (g) | (h) |
|---|---|---|---|---|---|---|---|---|
| Amount given | £5 | £5 | £5 | £5 | £10 | £10 | £20 | £20 |
| Cost of items | £3·22 | £2·74 | 35p | £2·07 | £8·13 | 77p | £8·06 | £17·73 |

**19** (a) Ranjit had 2 fish-fingers, salad, chips, yoghurt, and coffee at Pedro's Place (see Figure 5:16). How much should he pay?

Fig. 5:16

## Pedro's Place

| | | | |
|---|---|---|---|
| SAUSAGE | 30p | BREAD ROLL | 19p |
| FISH FINGER | 20p | BUTTER | 5p |
| FISH CAKE | 30p | CAKES (each) | 26p |
| PIZZA (slice) | 49p | YOGHURT | 30p |
| SALAD | 75p | COFFEE | 40p |
| CHIPS | 50p | TEA | 25p |
| BEEFBURGER | 48p | COKE | 45p |
| EGG | 22p | BISCUITS | 26p |
| BAKED POTATO | 45p | FRUIT | 24p |
| SOUP | 47p | MILK | 35p |

**TODAY'S SPECIAL** - THREE - COURSE MEAL £2·25

75
+40
5

Fig. 5:17

Manuel's meal
Soup
Bread roll
2 Sausage
Egg
Chips
Cake
Coke

Josie's meal
Soup
Pizza
Salad
Yoghurt
Fruit
Coffee

(b) Figure 5:17 shows what Manuel and Josie ate. Who pays the most? How much more?

(c) Mandy took her four friends to Pedro's Place for her birthday. They each had beefburger, salad, chips, cake, and coffee. Would Mandy be able to pay with her £10 note? If so, what change should she receive? If not, how much must she borrow from her friends?

(d) Can you choose a three-course meal (soup, main course, sweet, and drink) from the menu that costs the same as the Special Three-Course Meal?

20  You give a shopkeeper £5. To save change he asks you for a further 23p and then gives you 50p. What is the cost of the items you bought?

21  Look again at question 18. If you were the shopkeeper what would you ask the customer to give you if you were short of 1p and 2p coins?

22  (a)  The coins we use today are usually
        1p, 2p, 5p, 10p, 20p, 50p, £1.

        Suppose instead we used
        1p, 2p, 4p, 8p, 16p, 32p, 64p.

        Investigate using these coins for shopping.

    (b)  Suppose another country uses these coins:
        1p, 3p, 4p, 9p, 11p, 16p, 20p, 25p, 30p, 34p,
        39p, 41p, 46p, 47p, 49p, 50p.

        The people who use them say you can give any amount up to £1 using only two coins. Investigate.

## A Centre and radius

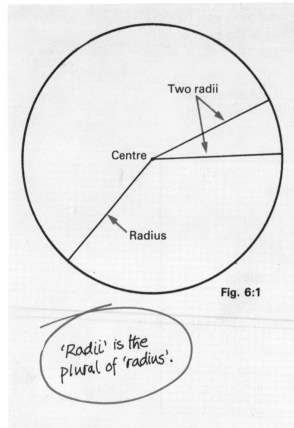

Fig. 6:1

'Radii' is the plural of 'radius'.

▶ **Points to discuss . . .**

1 > What do we mean by a circle?

2 > What objects have a circle in them?

3 > Figure 6:2 shows how to draw a circle on paper using compasses. How could you draw a large circle on the playground?

4 > How could you find the centre of a circular tea plate?

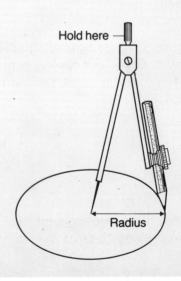

Hold here

Radius

Fig. 6:2

**1** Draw a circle of radius 5 cm. Then, using the same centre, draw four more circles of radii 4 cm, 3 cm, 2 cm, and 1 cm.

**2** (a) Copy Figure 6:3 exactly, leaving at least 3 cm space above and below it.

A       B       C       D       E       F       G

Fig. 6:3

(b) Draw five circles, each of radius 2 cm, with centres on the line at the points B, C, D, E and F.

(c) Repeat part (b), but use a radius of $1\frac{1}{2}$ cm.

(d) Colour or shade the rings to make your diagram look like a chain, as in Figure 6:4.

Fig. 6:4

**3** Copy Figure 6:5 exactly, leaving at least 2 cm space above and below it. Draw seven circles of radii $1\frac{1}{2}$ cm, with centres on the line at points B, C, D, E, F, G and H.

A       B       C       D       E       F       G       H       I

Fig. 6:5

Colour or shade your circles to look like a row of overlapping coins or counters.

**4** Copy Figure 6:6 exactly, leaving at least 4 cm space above and below it. Draw four circles, centres at B, C, D and E, all passing through the point A. The first two are shown in Figure 6:7.

A   B   C   D   E   F   G   H   I

Fig. 6:6

Then draw three circles, centres F, G and H, all passing through the point I.

A B C D E F G H I

Fig. 6:7

Worksheets 6A and 6B may be used here.

**5** Copy Figures 6:8 to 6:12, but make them twice as big. Use compasses for all circles and parts of circles. Centres are marked with dots. Always start with the biggest circle.

Colour the patterns.

Fig. 6:8

Fig. 6:9

Fig. 6:10

Fig. 6:11

Fig. 6:12

# B Diameter, circumference, arc and chord

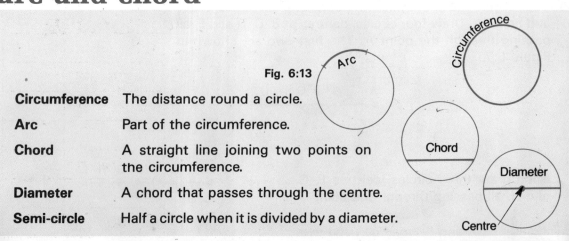

Fig. 6:13

| | |
|---|---|
| **Circumference** | The distance round a circle. |
| **Arc** | Part of the circumference. |
| **Chord** | A straight line joining two points on the circumference. |
| **Diameter** | A chord that passes through the centre. |
| **Semi-circle** | Half a circle when it is divided by a diameter. |

**1** Copy Figure 6:14, then copy and complete the table. The centre is marked O.

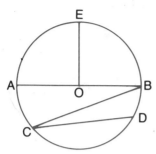

Fig. 6:14

| Line | Name |
|------|------|
| OA | Radius |
| OA, OE, OB | |
| AOB | |
| AC (curved) | |
| BC | |
| BE (curved) | |
| CD (straight) | |
| CD (curved) | |

**2** A circle has a radius of 4 cm. What length is its diameter?

**3** Figure 6:15 represents a coin being rolled through one complete turn. What length is the circumference of the coin?

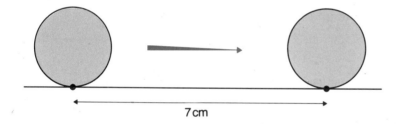

7 cm

Fig. 6:15

**4** Copy and complete the table for Figure 6:16.

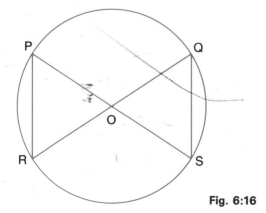

Fig. 6:16

| Line | Name |
|------|------|
| OP | Radius |
| QS (straight) | Cor |
| RS | curved Arc |
| QO | |
| OR, OS, OP | |
| PQ | |
| POS | |
| PR (straight) | |
| QOR | |
| OS, OQ | |

5  Copy and complete this table.

| Radius | 13 cm | 17 cm | | | $6\frac{1}{2}$ cm |
|---|---|---|---|---|---|
| Diameter | 26 cm | | 88 cm | 48 cm | |

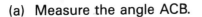

| Radius | $8\frac{1}{2}$ cm | $16\frac{1}{2}$ cm | ×2 | | |
|---|---|---|---|---|---|
| Diameter | ÷2 | | 11 cm | 23 cm | 92 cm |

6  Draw a picture (not a pattern) using only straight lines, circles and arcs.

7  Draw any circle. Draw a diameter AB. Mark any point C on the circumference. Join A to C and B to C. You should have a diagram like Figure 6:17. Mark a point D on your diagram in about the same place as the point D in Figure 6:17.

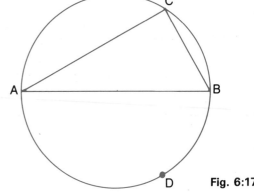

Fig. 6:17

(a)  Measure the angle ACB.

(b)  Now join D to A and B and measure angle ADB. What do you notice?

(c)  Investigate what happens if you take other positions for C or D.

8  Copy and complete the following sentences with the names for parts of a circle.

(a)  The boundary of a circle is its . . .

(b)  Part of the boundary of a circle is called an . . .

(c)  Half a circle is called a . . .

(d)  A straight line which passes through the centre of a circle is called a . . .

(e)  A straight line which joins the centre to the circumference is called a . . .

(f)  The radius of a circle is half the length of its . . .

(g)  A straight line which divides a circle into two unequal parts is called a . . .

Do not write on the book!

9  The ball (or sphere) in Figure 6:18 has a set of parallel
   lines painted on it. Draw a picture of the sphere seen from
   directly above it.

**Fig. 6:18**

10 Figure 6:19 represents a sphere of plasticine which is to
   be sliced through AB, BC and BD.

   (a)  Into how many pieces will the sphere be cut?

   (b)  What shape will the flat parts of the pieces be?

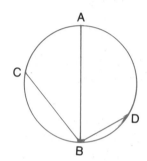

**Fig. 6:19**

11 Draw a set of concentric (same-centred) circles of radii
   1 cm, 2 cm, 3 cm, 4 cm, 5 cm and 6 cm. Draw a diameter
   of the 6 cm circle. Draw ten chords parallel (like exercise-
   book lines) to the diameter and spaced 1 cm apart.
   Colour every other section of your pattern black.

# Metric system: length

## A Centimetre and millimetre

centimetres (cm)

Fig. 7:1

A **centimetre** is one hundredth ($\frac{1}{100}$) of a metre. Centimetre is shortened to **cm**.

millimetres (mm)

Fig. 7:2

A **millimetre** is one thousandth ($\frac{1}{1000}$) of a metre. Millimetre is shortened to **mm**.

$$1 \, cm = 10 \, mm \qquad 1 \, mm = \tfrac{1}{10} \, cm = 0 \cdot 1 \, cm$$

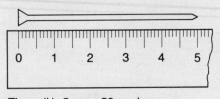 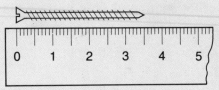

Fig. 7:3

The nail is 5 cm or 50 mm long.     The screw is 3·5 cm or 35 mm long.

**1** How long are the objects in Figure 7:4? You should try to answer both in cm and in mm, as in Figure 7:3.

(a)

 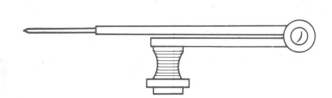

(b)

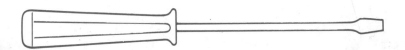

Fig. 7:4 *cont.*

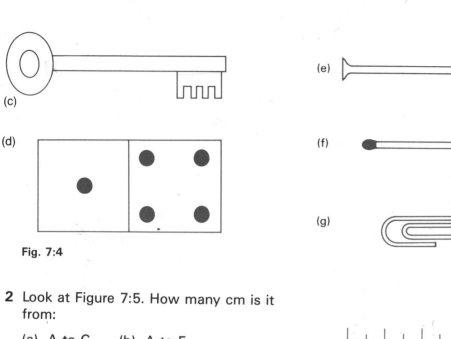

(c)

(d)

(e)

(f)

(g)

**Fig. 7:4**

**2** Look at Figure 7:5. How many cm is it from:

(a)  A to C       (b)  A to E

(c)  B to D       (d)  C to F?

A      B      C      D      E      F

**Fig. 7:5**

**3** Look at Figure 7:5. How many mm is it from:

(a)  A to B       (b)  A to D       (c)  B to E       (d)  F to C?

**4** In Figure 7:6, line (a) is $3\frac{1}{2}$ cm long. Check this, then copy the lines and write on your copies how long each line is in cm.

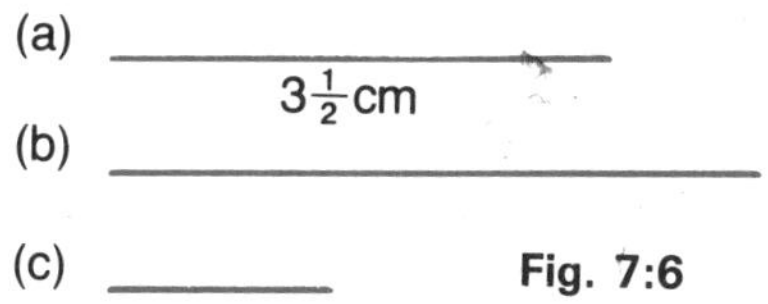

(a) _____
$3\frac{1}{2}$ cm

(b) _____

(c) _____       **Fig. 7:6**

**5** In Figure 7:7, line (a) is 23 mm long. Check this, then copy the lines and write on your copies how long each line is in mm.

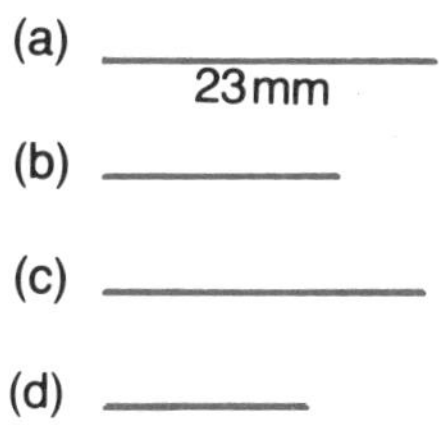

(a) _____
23 mm

(b) _____

(c) _____

(d) _____       **Fig. 7:7**

How many mm make:

(a)  1 cm 2 mm       (b)  2 cm 6 mm       (c)  3·5 cm

(d)  4·8 cm       (e)  12·4 cm?

**7 Example** 24 mm is 2 cm 4 mm.

Copy and complete these like the example.

(a) 28 mm is . . .    (b) 47 mm is . . .

(c) 89 mm is . . .    (d) 125 mm is . . .

(e) 360 mm is . . .

**8 Remember** 10 mm = 1 cm, so 1 mm = $\frac{1}{10}$ cm or 0·1 cm.

The tenths ($\frac{1}{10}$ or 0·1) column is the first column after the decimal point.

**Example** 8 mm = $\frac{8}{10}$ cm or 0·8 cm

Copy and complete these like the example.

(a) 2 mm =    (b) 4 mm =    (c) 7 mm =

**9 Example** 24 mm = 2·4 cm

Copy and complete these like the example.

(a) 32 mm =    (b) 53 mm =    (c) 156 mm =

(d) 203 mm =    (e) 666 mm =    (f) 108 mm =

(g) 317 mm =    (h) 200 mm =    (i) 5000 mm =

**10** How many millimetres make:

(a) 6·9 cm    (b) 4·3 cm    (c) 16·9 cm

(d) 18·2 cm    (e) 20·4 cm    (f) 30·5 cm?

**11** Draw as accurately as you can a line of length:

(a) 22 mm    (b) 2·4 cm    (c) 18 mm    (d) 2 cm    (e) 2 mm

**12** Write the measurements in question 11 in order of size, starting with the smallest.

**13** Without drawing lines, write the following measurements in order of size from smallest to largest.

(a) 14 cm,  12 mm,  9 mm,  3·6 cm,  111 mm

(b) 3 mm,  3 cm,  33 mm,  3·1 cm,  31 cm

(c) 11 cm,  105 mm,  10·1 cm,  10 cm,  111 mm

**14** The goldfish in Figure 7:8 is 4 cm long.
It grows longer by 3 mm each year.

Copy this table and complete it to show
how the fish grows for the next five
years.

0 cm    1    2    3    4    **Fig. 7:8**

| When | Length |
|---|---|
| Now | 4 cm 0 mm = 4·0 cm = 40 mm |
| After 1 year | 4 cm 3 mm = 4·3 cm = 43 mm |
| After 2 years | |
| After 3 years | |
| After 4 years | |
| After 5 years | |

**15** Figure 7:9 shows some measurements that were used a
long time ago. Compare your digit, span and cubit with
your teacher's. Write a sentence saying why using these
as measures is not a very good idea.

**Digit**

The widest part of
your index finger

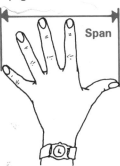

**Span**

Your handspan
(fingers outstretched)

**Cubit**

The distance from your elbow
to the tip of your fingers

**Fig. 7:9**

**16** Find out about measurements that are not metric. What
other measurements were used in the past? Which of
them are still being used? When do you use non-metric
measurements? You could make a wall display of your
answers, with pictures and examples.

# B Centimetre and metre

**1** Example $5\frac{1}{2}$ m = 550 cm

Copy and complete these like the example.

(a) 2 m =    (b) 7 m =    (c) 12 m =

(d) $\frac{1}{2}$ m =    (e) 6 m 17 cm =

**2** Example 370 cm = 3·70 m

Copy and complete these like the example.

(a) 128 cm =    (b) 160 cm =    (c) 275 cm =

(d) 270 cm =

**3** If you measured the length of a match you would probably use mm.

Would you use mm, cm, or m to measure:

(a) the length of a pin

(b) the length of a new pencil

(c) the height of a flag pole

(d) the length of a cricket bat

(e) the height of a milk bottle

(f) the thickness of a £1 coin?

**4** Choose the most likely measurement from the list given:

(a) length of a pin: 25 cm, 2 mm, 25 mm, 25 m

(b) length of a swimming pool: 2·5 cm, 25 mm, 25 m, 2 cm

(c) length of a pair of compasses: 9 m, 9 mm, 90 cm, 9·5 cm

(d) length of a car: 36 cm, 36 m, 3·6 m, 36 mm

**5 Example** $2\frac{1}{2}$ m = 250 cm

Copy and complete these like the example.

(a) 3 m =          (b) 5 m =          (c) 9 m =

(d) $1\frac{1}{2}$ m =          (e) $3\frac{1}{2}$ m =          (f) $5\frac{1}{2}$ m =

(g) 0·5 m =          (h) 10 m =          (i) $10\frac{1}{2}$ m =

**6** How many cm make:

(a) 3 m 14 cm          (b) 3 m 4 cm          (c) 10 m 6 cm

(d) 10 m 10 cm?

**7 Remember**   100 cm = 1 m, so 1 cm = $\frac{1}{100}$ m or 0·01 m

The hundredths ($\frac{1}{100}$) column is the second column after the decimal point.

**Example**   (i)  309 cm = 3·09 m
(ii)  2 m 25 cm = 2·25 m

Copy and complete these like the example.

(a)  208 cm =          (b)  145 cm =          (c)  333 cm =

(d)  300 cm =          (e)  3 m 45 cm =

(f)  2 m 5 cm =          (g)  10 m 10 cm =

**8** Figure 7:10 shows a garden shed. What is its length? Answer in metres and centimetres (like 5 m 8 cm).

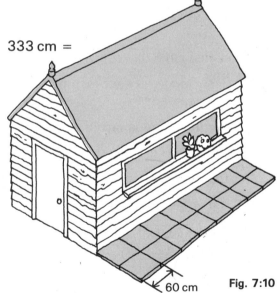

60 cm          **Fig. 7:10**

**9** Figure 7:11 shows a picture. What total length of wood is needed to make the frame? Answer in metres and centimetres.

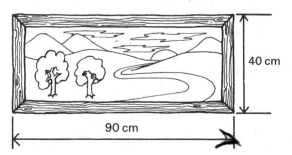

40 cm

90 cm

**Fig. 7:11**

**10** Figure 7:12 shows a fence made entirely of wood. What length of wood is needed altogether? Answer in metres and centimetres.

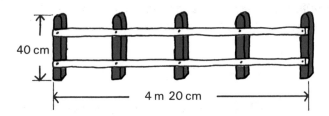

40 cm

4 m 20 cm

**Fig. 7:12**

**11** Figure 7:13 shows a chimney-sweeping brush. As the brush is pushed up the chimney it is made longer by screwing on another rod. Each new rod makes it 75 cm longer. The brush rod is 100 cm long.

**Fig. 7:13**

(a) How long will the brush be when four rods have been screwed on?

(b) How many rods would you need to clean a chimney 5 m high?

**12** Timber is sold in lengths of 30 cm, 60 cm, 90 cm, 120 cm and every 30 cm to 360 cm. 1 foot is about 30·5 cm.

If you want to buy 4 feet of timber, you need 4 × 30·5 cm = 122 cm.
You will have to buy 150 cm which is 28 cm too much.

Make a table to show what lengths in centimetres you would have to buy if you needed 1 foot, 2 feet, 3 feet and so on up to 10 feet. Show in your table how much extra you would have.

# C Kilometre

In Britain, Canada and the USA, large distances on land are usually measured in **miles**. In European countries a unit of measure called the **kilometre** (**km** for short) is used. A kilometre is a smaller distance than a mile. In fact, 1 mile is about 1·6 km.

## ▶ Points to discuss . . .

1> Would it be a good idea for everyone to measure long distances in kilometres instead of miles?

2> The distance round an athletics track is 400 metres. Each straight is 100 metres long.

1 kilometre = 1000 metres.

(a) How many 100 m races will you have to run to travel 1 km?

(b) How many laps of the track will you have to run to travel 1 km?

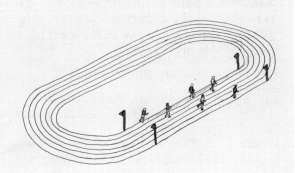

1 Figure 7:14 shows a map of some villages. How far is it in metres from:

(a) Anton to Beacon

(b) Beacon to Catby

(c) Catby to Denton

(d) Denton to Eptown

(e) Eptown to Anton?

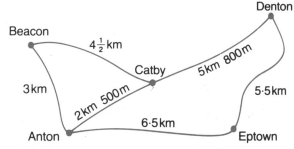

Fig. 7:14

2

| School Sports Meeting |
| --- |
| 1500 metres 2 p.m. |
| 3000 metres 2:30 p.m. |
| 5000 metres 3:15 p.m. |

Copy this notice, changing the distances into kilometres.

**3** Figure 7:15 shows a map. The distances are in metres. How far is it in **kilometres** from:

(a) Fenton to Gilby      (b) Gilby to Horton

(c) Gilby to Intdown      (d) Fenton to Intdown?

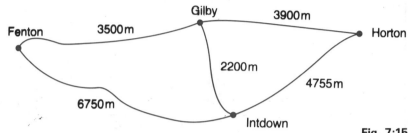

Fig. 7:15

**4 Examples**   1 km = 1000 m,   $\frac{1}{2}$ km = 500 m,
$\frac{1}{4}$ km = 250 m

Copy and complete the following like the examples.

(a) $1\frac{1}{4}$ km =      (b) $2\frac{1}{4}$ km =      (c) $3\frac{3}{4}$ km =

(d) $5\frac{3}{4}$ km =      (e) $\frac{1}{8}$ km =

What do you think 'kilo' means?

**5** Figure 7:16 shows a map of Reuben's journey to school. How far is Reuben's journey in:

(a) metres      (b) kilometres?

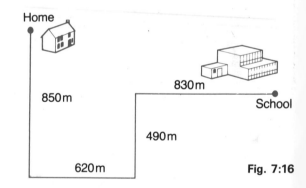

Fig. 7:16

**6** Figure 7:17 shows some towns near to Melanie's home in Upton. The distances are in kilometres. How far does Melanie drive when she drives from Upton through Lowton to Highton, then on through Stanton to Churchton? Give your answer in:

(a) kilometres      (b) metres

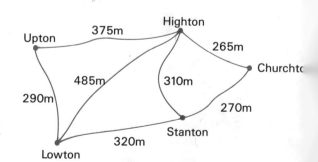

Fig. 7:17

**7** Figure 7:18 shows a model railway track in a fun park. Copy Figure 7:19 (you could draw round a coin for the circles) and complete it to show the distances of each station from A.

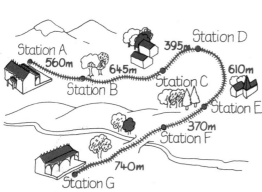

Fig. 7:18

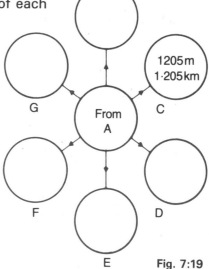

Fig. 7:19

**8** Make a poster showing objects you would measure in kilometres, metres, centimetres and millimetres. Write a suitable size for each object.

850
620
490
830
2020

290
375
270
4 3 5

# Integers and decimals: multiplication

## A Multiplication by single integers

Multiplication is a quick way to add lots of the same number.

$3 + 3 + 3 + 3 + 3 + 3 + 3 + 3 = 24$     $8 \times 3 = 24$

To find how many tablets there are in Figure 8:1 you do not need to count every one. There are 3 rows of 4, so there are $3 \times 4 = 12$ tablets.

Fig. 8:1

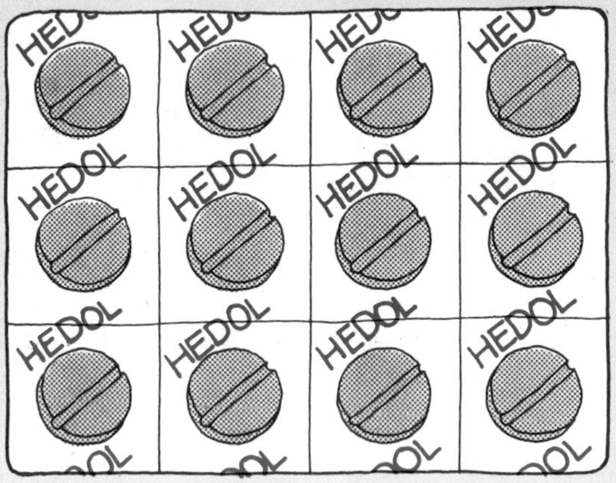

| × | 3 | 4 |
|---|---|---|
| 3 | 9 | 12 |
| 4 | 12 | 16 |

**A multiplication square**

× 2

| | | |
|---|---|---|
| 3 | ⟶ | 6 |
| 8 | ⟶ | 16 |
| 9 | ⟶ | 18 |

**A multiplication link**

**1** (a) $5 + 5 + 5 + 5 + 5 + 5$

(b) $6 + 6 + 6 + 6 + 6 + 6 + 6 + 6$

(c) $8 + 8 + 8 + 8 + 8$

(d) $9 + 9 + 9 + 9 + 9 + 9 + 9 + 9 + 9 + 9$

**2** The order in which numbers are multiplied does not matter.

(a) $7 \times 9$ is 63. What is $9 \times 7$?

(b) $8 \times 13$ is 104. What is $13 \times 8$?

(c) $19 \times 4$ is 76. What is $4 \times 19$?

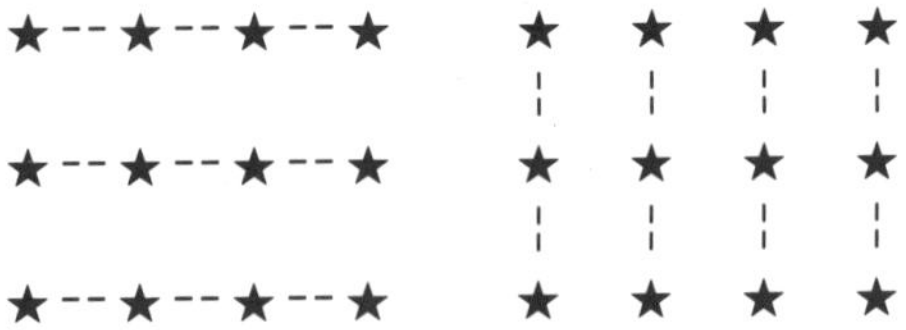

$3 \times 4 = 12$     $4 \times 3 = 12$

**3** Copy and complete these multiplication squares.

(a)

| × | 5 | 6 |
|---|---|---|
| 5 | | |
| 6 | | |

(b)

| × | 3 | 6 | 7 |
|---|---|---|---|
| 3 | | | |
| 6 | | | |
| 7 | | | |

(c)

| × | 4 | 8 | 9 |
|---|---|---|---|
| 2 | | | |
| 6 | | | |
| 7 | | | |

**4** Copy and complete these multiplication links.

(a)  × 2

| 2 | → | |
| 7 | → | |
| 5 | → | |

(b)  × 4

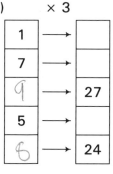

| 3 | → | |
| 6 | → | |
| 4 | → | |

(c)  × 6

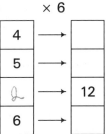

| 4 | → | |
| 5 | → | |
| 2 | → | 12 |
| 6 | → | |

(d)  × 7

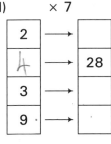

| 2 | → | |
| 4 | → | 28 |
| 3 | → | |
| 9 · | → | |

(e)  × 3

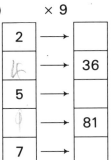

| 1 | → | |
| 7 | → | |
| 9 | → | 27 |
| 5 | → | |
| 8 | → | 24 |

(f)  × 5

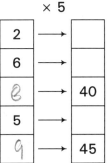

| 2 | → | |
| 6 | → | |
| 8 | → | 40 |
| 5 | → | |
| 9 | → | 45 |

(g)  × 8

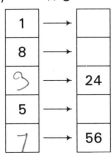

| 1 | → | |
| 8 | → | |
| 3 | → | 24 |
| 5 | → | |
| 7 | → | 56 |

(h)  × 9

| 2 | → | |
| 4 | → | 36 |
| 5 | → | |
| 9 | → | 81 |
| 7 | → | |

Worksheet 8A may be used here.

**5**          **4 × 3**
is the same as 4 + 4 + 4.
is the same as 3 + 3 + 3 + 3.
means '3 lots of 4'.
means '4 lots of 3'.
is said '4 multiplied by 3'.
is said '3 multiplied by 4'.
is '4 increased 3 times'.
is '3 increased 4 times'.
is the **product** of 4 and 3.
is the product of 3 and 4.

Write what 5 × 4 means in as many ways as you can.

**6 Example** Calculate 4 × 13.

13 = 3 + 10    4 lots of 3  = 12 ⎫
                        4 lots of 10 = 40 ⎬ Add
                        4 lots of 13 = 52 ⎭

It is easier to write it like this:

```
      13
    ×  4
      12 ⎫
      40 ⎬ Add
      52
```

(a)　　16　　(b)　　15　　(c)　　18　　(d)　　19　　(e)　　23
　　× 3　　　　× 5　　　　× 2　　　　× 4　　　　× 3

**7** (a)　　24　　(b)　　35　　(c)　　47　　(d)　　58　　(e)　　69
　　× 4　　　　× 5　　　　× 3　　　　× 2　　　　× 5

**8** (a)　　60　　(b)　　70　　(c)　　50　　(d)　　40　　(e)　　30
　　× 2　　　　× 3　　　　× 4　　　　× 7　　　　× 8

**9** (a)　　123　　(b)　　127　　(c)　　216　　(d)　　134　　(e)　　156
　　× 3　　　　　× 4　　　　　× 6　　　　　× 5　　　　　× 3

**10** (a)　　27　　(b)　　68　　(c)　　45　　(d)　　59　　(e)　　36
　　× 7　　　　× 8　　　　× 7　　　　× 8　　　　× 7

**11** (a)　　89　　(b)　　99　　(c)　　187　　(d)　　198　　(e)　　167
　　× 8　　　　× 9　　　　× 8　　　　× 9　　　　× 7

**12** (a)　　206　　(b)　　308　　(c)　　406　　(d)　　103　　(e)　　108
　　× 3　　　　　× 2　　　　　× 4　　　　　× 5　　　　　× 6

**13** (a) 97 × 8　　(b) 88 × 7　　(c) 170 × 7

　　(d) 106 × 7　　(e) 89 × 9

**14** Find the missing number.

(a) $6 \times 7 = \square$  (b) $8 \times \square = 48$  (c) $\square \times 6 = 24$

(d) $56 = 8 \times \square$  (e) $32 = \square \times 4$  (f) $64 = 8 \times \square$

(g) $7 \times 16 = \square$  (h) $\square = 17 \times 9$  (i) $8 \times 16 = \square$

You may use a calculator for the following questions.

**15** Curtain hooks are packed 24 to a box. How many are in 6 boxes?

**16** A tray contains 36 eggs. How many are in 8 trays?

**17** What is the product of 58 and 7?

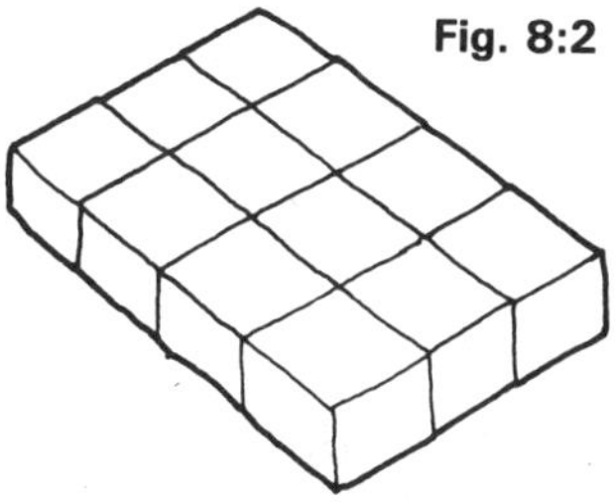

**18** A block of fudge is divided into 3 rows, 4 pieces to a row. How many pieces are there in 7 whole blocks?

Fig. 8:2

**19** My heart beats 68 times in 1 minute. About how many times will it beat in 8 minutes?

**20** Tablets are packaged on cards, each of which has 4 rows of 7 tablets. How many tablets are in a box of 9 cards?

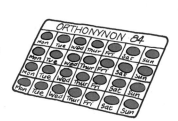

**21** A rugby team has 15 players. How many players are needed to make up 7 teams?

Fig. 8:3

**22** A manager employs 58 workers. She pays each of them £25 a day.

(a) How much is her wage bill per day?

(b) How much is her wage bill per week?

**23** A sliced loaf has 27 slices. If a guest house buys 3 loaves each day, how many slices will they have bought in:

(a) a day  (b) a week?

Worksheet 8B may be used here.

**24** 5 × 7 × 8 can be calculated in three ways:

(i) 35 × 8     (ii) 5 × 56     (iii) 40 × 7

Which is easiest to do in your head?

Find the easiest way to work out:

(a) 5 × 9 × 6     (b) 7 × 5 × 4     (c) 9 × 8 × 5

(d) 8 × 2 × 15     (e) 2 × 7 × 5     (f) 6 × 7 × 5

(g) 15 × 4 × 5     (h) 2 × 18 × 5

**25** Use the numbers on a clockface.

(a) Find which two numbers give the smallest product.

(b) Find which two numbers give the largest product.

(c) Write all the pairs of numbers which have a product greater than 42.

(d) Find which three numbers have a product smaller than 20.

(e) Find which three numbers have a product of 864.

# B Multiplication by tens, hundreds and thousands

Sue and Sam worked out 700 × 300 in different ways. Which way do you think is better?

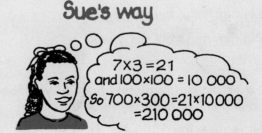

Sam's way

700
×300
000
0000
210000
210000

Sue's way

7×3 = 21
and 100×100 = 10 000
So 700×300 = 21×10 000
= 210 000

Fig. 8:4

**1** Copy and complete this table.

| Number | 5 | 12 | 1 | 24 | 20 | 48 | 0 | 100 |
|--------|---|----|---|----|----|----|---|-----|
| × 1 | | | | | | | | |
| × 10 | | | | | | | | |
| × 100 | | | | | | | | |
| × 1000 | | | | | | | | |

**2** (a) 3 × 10　　(b) 60 × 4　　(c) 20 × 40

　　(d) 300 × 5　　(e) 60 × 40　　(f) 700 × 80

**3** (a) 40 × 800　　(b) 700 × 700　　(c) 80 × 90 000

　　(d) 500 × 20　　(e) 100 × 100　　(f) 60 × 70

**4** (a) 50 × 40　　(b) 1000 × 0 (Careful!)

　　(c) 70 × 8000　　(d) 500 × 60　　(e) 500 × 400

　　(f) 1000 × 1000 × 1000 (a billion)

**5** The rectangle in Figure 8:5 has 20 columns of 14 small squares, that is 20 lots of 14 squares. How many small squares are there?

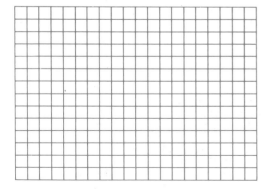

**Fig. 8:5**

**6** Find how many small squares there are in each rectangle in
Figure 8:6.

(a)

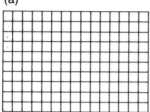

(b)

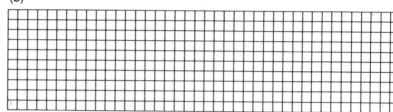

(c)

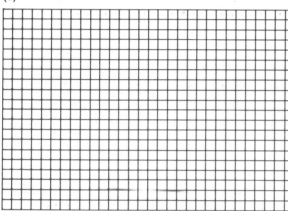

Fig. 8:6

**7** State the missing numbers.

(a) $\square \times 10 = 70$      (b) $\square \times 100 = 500$

(c) $\square \times 10 = 360$      (d) $\square \times 100 = 2700$

(e) $6 \times \square = 60$      (f) $17 \times \square = 170$

**8** Find the value of each letter.

(a) $36 \times a = 3600$      (b) $48 \times 100 = b$

(c) $360 \times 10 = c$      (d) $100 \times d = 2700$

(e) $e \times 50 = 1000$      (f) $1000 \times f = 0$

**9** What is the product of:

(a) 10 and 10 (the answer is *not* 20)      (b) 10 and 100

(c) 100 and 1      (d) 100 and 100

(e) 10 and 10 and 10      (f) 1000 and 1

(g) 1 000 000 000 000 000 000 and 0?

**10**  A gardener plants 20 rows of lettuces, 30 plants to the row. How many lettuces does he plant?

**11**  A theatre has 80 rows, each having 50 seats. How many seats are there in the theatre?

**12**  Nikita has 12 metres of wire. How many 2 metre lengths can he cut?

**13**  Nadia cuts 200 ribbons, each 80 cm long, from a reel. How much ribbon was on the reel to start with if it is now empty?

**14**  Jerome changes £1 into 10p tokens for a fruit machine. Each token gives him one game. He plays 17 games, and then has no tokens left. How many tokens did he win?

**15**  A shop display of baked bean cans is in a triangle shape, with 10 cans on the bottom row, 9 on the next row, and so on to the top row with 1 can only.

(a)  How many rows of cans are there?

(b)  How many cans are there?

**16**  A million is written 1 000 000.

1 000 000 can also be written as 10 × 100 000.

Using only 0s and 1s, how many different ways can you write a million?

**17**  You need a sheet of graph paper. Find out how many small squares there are on it. How many sheets of graph paper would you need for a million small squares? Is your classroom wall big enough to hold a million of these squares? (If you really want a challenge, how many squares of any size are on your piece of graph paper?)

# C Multiplication by two-digit numbers

Morag can do the first calculation because she knows her multiplication tables.

Fig. 8:7

She can do the second calculation by saying '6 lots of 3 make 18 and 10 lots of 6 make 60, and 18 + 60 is 78'.

But she cannot do the third calculation in her head because she does not know her 23 times table. She can do it by writing it like this:

```
      28
   ×  23
      84   This is 28 × 3.
     560   This is 28 × 20.
     644
```

**1** (a)   24       (b)   23      (c)   26      (d)   31
         × 21           × 32          × 21          × 32

  (e)   22
      × 42

**2** (a)   16       (b)   18      (c)   19      (d)   26
         × 20           × 30          × 40          × 20

  (e)   36
      × 30

**3** (a) 36 × 21    (b) 42 × 31    (c) 43 × 32

  (d) 52 × 43    (e) 33 × 44

4 (a) 27 × 32    (b) 46 × 14    (c) 39 × 15

  (d) 47 × 52    (e) 69 × 34

5 Always make sure that your answers are sensible.
  29 × 19 is about 30 × 20, which is 600.
  So if you write 29 × 19 = 290 you should look for your
  mistake.

  Suggest an approximate answer for:

  (a) 19 × 19    (b) 28 × 21    (c) 42 × 31

  (d) 99 × 38    (e) 47 × 101    (f) 68 × 19

  (g) 198 × 79    (h) 997 × 61

6 Use your calculator to work out the exact answers to question 5. Compare your answers with your approximate
  ones.

---

7 Here are two checks that will tell you if you have made
  a mistake in multiplication. (They cannot tell you your
  answer is **right** though. You may like to think about why
  this is.)

  **Check one    Last digit**

  For 56 × 43 the last digit must be 8, as 6 × 3 = 18, and
  8 is the last digit of 18. You can see why this works if you
  think of the multiplication set out as usual:

```
      56
  ×   43
     168   The last digit is 8.
    2240   The last digit is always 0.
    2408   8 + 0 = 8
```

  **Check two    Digit sum**

  1. Find the digit sum of both numbers in the question.

  2. Multiply these digit sums.

  3. Find the digit sum of the answer to step 2.

  4. The answer to step 3 should be the same as the digit
     sum of your final answer.

**Example**

$56 \times 43 = 2408$

The digit sum of 56 is $5 + 6 = 11 \to$ **2** $\Big\}$ $2 \times 7 = 14$
The digit sum of 43 is $4 + 3 = 7 \to$ **7** $\Big\}$ $1 + 4 = 5$ $\Big\}$ These are
The digit sum of 2408 is $2 + 4 + 0 + 8 = 14 \to$ **5** $\Big\}$ the same.

Use both checks to find out which of the following are wrong:

(a) $14 \times 23 = 322$     (b) $25 \times 32 = 800$

(c) $17 \times 16 = 282$     (d) $41 \times 33 = 1553$

(e) $57 \times 35 = 2052$     (f) $62 \times 29 = 1768$

(g) $38 \times 25 = 960$     (h) $84 \times 76 = 6384$

(i) $53 \times 22 = 1166$     (j) $48 \times 17 = 817$

(k) $33 \times 29 = 957$     (l) $44 \times 67 = 2946$

# D Decimal fractions: multiplication by tens, hundreds and thousands

This drawing pin is $0 \cdot 8$ cm long.

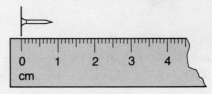

Fig. 8:8

Here are ten drawing pins placed end to end.

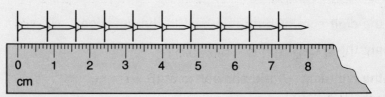

Fig. 8:9

The total length of the ten pins is $0 \cdot 8$ cm $\times 10 = 8$ cm.

**1** Look at Figure 8:10. What is the total length of ten of the insects placed nose to tail?

0·4 cm  Fig. 8:10

**2** If ten drawing pins each 0·8 cm long are placed end to end the total length is 0·8 cm × 10 = 8 cm.

If a hundred drawing pins were placed end to end they would stretch ten times further than ten drawing pins, because a hundred is ten tens.

0·8 cm × 10 = 8 cm
0·8 cm × 100 = 80 cm

Look at the washer in Figure 8:11.

(a) What is the total length of ten washers placed touching each other in a straight line?

(b) What is the total length of a hundred washers placed touching each other in a straight line?

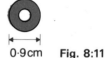

0·9 cm    Fig. 8:11

**3** If a thousand drawing pins are placed end to end their total length is ten times longer than a hundred drawing pins, because a thousand is ten times a hundred.

0·8 cm × 10    =    8 cm
0·8 cm × 100   =   80 cm
0·8 cm × 1000 = 800 cm

Look at Figure 8:12. What is the total length of 1000 of the screws placed end to end?

0·7 cm    Fig. 8:12

**4** Look at Figure 8:13. The nail is 1·2 cm long.
Figure 8:14 shows ten of the nails placed end to end.

1·2 cm    Fig. 8:13

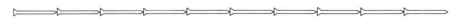

Fig. 8:14

(a) What is the total length of the ten nails?

(b) How far would a hundred nails stretch? (Remember that 100 = 10 × 10.)

(c) How far would a thousand nails stretch? (Remember that 1000 = 100 × 10.)

**5** In answering questions 1 to 4, did you notice the following?

Multiplying by 10 moves the figures one column to the left, making them worth ten times as much.

|  | 100 | 10 | 1 | $\frac{1}{10}$ | $\frac{1}{100}$ | $\frac{1}{1000}$ |
|---|---|---|---|---|---|---|
| 0·8 |  |  | 0 · 8 |  |  |  |
| 0·8 × 10 |  |  | 8 · |  |  |  |

Multiplying by 100 moves the figures two columns to the left, making them worth a hundred times as much.

|  | 100 | 10 | 1 | $\frac{1}{10}$ | $\frac{1}{100}$ | $\frac{1}{1000}$ |
|---|---|---|---|---|---|---|
| 0·8 |  |  | 0 · 8 |  |  |  |
| 0·8 × 100 |  | 8 | 0 · |  |  |  |

Multiplying by 1000 moves the figures three columns to the left, making them worth a thousand times as much.

|  | 100 | 10 | 1 | $\frac{1}{10}$ | $\frac{1}{100}$ | $\frac{1}{1000}$ |
|---|---|---|---|---|---|---|
| 0·8 |  |  | 0 · 8 |  |  |  |
| 0·8 × 1000 | 8 | 0 | 0 · |  |  |  |

Copy and complete these tables.

(a)

| Number | 6 | 6·1 | 6·12 | 61 | 61·2 | 0·6 | 0·61 | 0·612 |
|---|---|---|---|---|---|---|---|---|
| × 10 |  |  |  |  |  |  |  |  |
| × 100 |  |  |  |  |  |  |  |  |

(b)

| Number | 7 | 7·9 | 7·95 | 79 | 79·5 | 0·7 | 0·79 | 0·795 |
|---|---|---|---|---|---|---|---|---|
| × 10 |  |  |  |  |  |  |  |  |
| × 100 |  |  |  |  |  |  |  |  |
| × 1000 |  |  |  |  |  |  |  |  |

**6** Find the missing numbers:

(a) $6 \cdot 4 \times \square = 64$      (b) $8 \cdot 32 \times \square = 83 \cdot 2$

(c) $7 \cdot 16 \times \square = 716$      (d) $4 \cdot 65 \times \square = 46 \cdot 5$

(e) $0 \cdot 415 \times \square = 41 \cdot 5$      (f) $4 \cdot 15 \times \square = 4150$

(g) $\square \times 2 \cdot 8 = 28$      (h) $\square \times 15 \cdot 6 = 15 \cdot 6$

(i) $\square \times 0 \cdot 135 = 135$

Fig. 8:15

← 2·2 cm →

**7** A pound coin is $2 \cdot 2$ cm wide.

(a) How long will a line of 100 £1 coins be?

(b) How much will the line of coins be worth?

**8** A matchbox is $4 \cdot 8$ cm long.

(a) How long will a line of 100 matchboxes be?

(b) How long will a line of 1000 matchboxes be?

Fig. 8:16

4·8 cm

**9** A garden fence panel is $1 \cdot 9$ metres long.

(a) How long a fence will 10 panels make?

(b) What will the 10 panels cost at £$8 \cdot 20$ each?

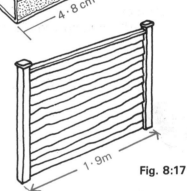

1·9m

Fig. 8:17

**10** A sheet of paper is $0 \cdot 12$ mm thick.

(a) What is the thickness of a pile of 100 sheets of paper?

(b) A ream of paper is 500 sheets. What is the thickness of a ream of this paper?

(c) A ream of paper costs £$2 \cdot 05$. What is the cost of ten reams?

Fig. 8:18

**11** A calculator is said to have 'a floating point'. Why?

**12** Draw a square metre on the floor or playground. How many pupils can stand comfortably inside the square? How many could stand in a kilometre square?

# A Naming polygons

A **polygon** is a plane (flat) shape with any number of straight sides.

Some polygons have special names. For example:

| | | | |
|---|---|---|---|
| triangle | 3 sides | heptagon | 7 sides |
| quadrilateral | 4 sides | octagon | 8 sides |
| pentagon | 5 sides | nonagon | 9 sides |
| hexagon | 6 sides | decagon | 10 sides |

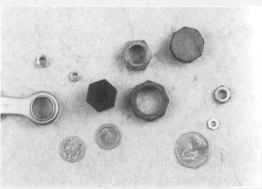

Figure 9:1 shows a **convex** and a **concave** polygon.

Convex polygon       Concave polygon      **Fig. 9:1**

If all the sides and all the angles are equal, the shape is called
a **regular** polygon. All the polygons in Figure 9:2 are regular.
The polygons in Figure 9:1 are **irregular**.

Equilateral triangle

Square

Regular pentagon

**Fig. 9:2**       Regular hexagon

**1** Name the following polygons in Figure 9:3.

(a) The spire of the clock tower

(b) The window with the bell, in the spire

(c) The door in the clock tower

(d) The clock

(e) The windows on the side

(f) The window in the small tower

(g) The whole shape (right round the outside)     **Fig. 9:3**

**2** Copy each shape in Figure 9:4. You can make then bigger, but keep them as nearly the same shape as you can. Write the correct name under each one, chosen from the following list.

Triangle   Concave quadrilateral   Convex quadrilateral
Concave pentagon   Convex pentagon
Concave hexagon   Convex hexagon   Concave octagon
Convex octagon   Concave decagon

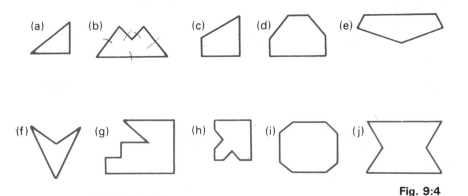

**Fig. 9:4**

**3** Follow the instructions given in Figures 9:5 and 9:6. Write on the polygon you cut its name, then stick it in your book.

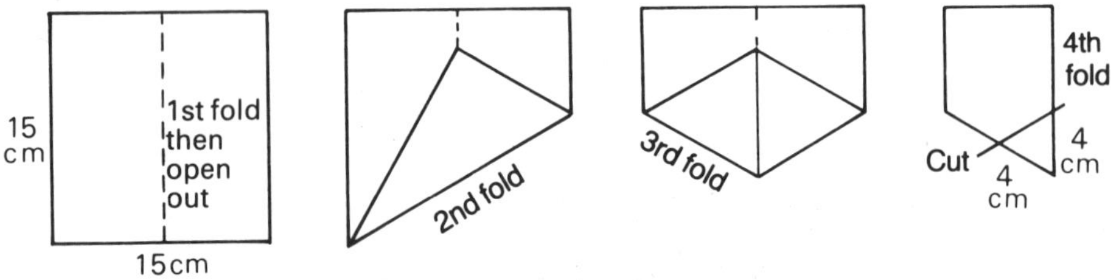

**Fig. 9:5**

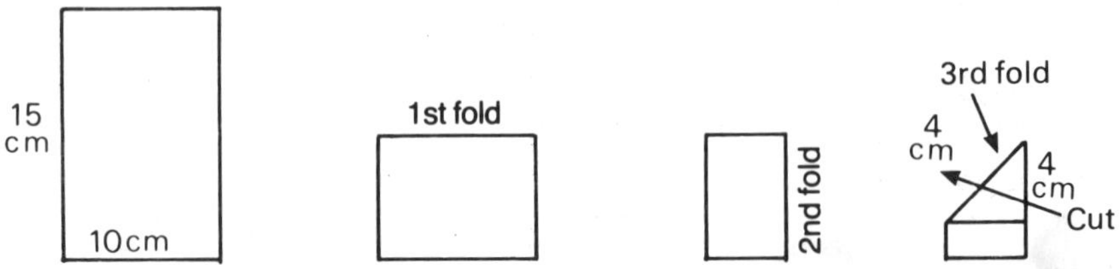

**Fig. 9:6**

Worksheets 9A and 9B may be used here.

# B Drawing regular polygons

Regular polygons have all sides and angles equal.

Figure 9:7 shows how to draw a regular hexagon.

(a) Draw a circle around the circumference of a circular protractor.

(b) Divide the circumference of your circle into six equal parts (360° ÷ 6 = 60°).

(c) Join each point to the next point.

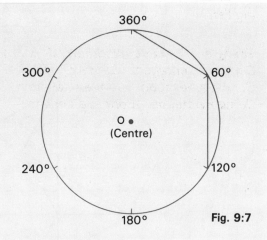

Fig. 9:7

1 In Figure 9:8, ABCDEF is a regular hexagon.

(a) What size is angle DOC (the angle at the centre)?

(b) What kind of triangle is triangle DOC?

2 Copy and complete this table, then draw the regular polygons. Use the angles at the centre to divide the circumferences into the correct number of parts.

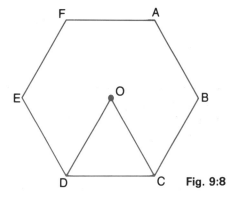

Fig. 9:8

| Number of sides | Name of regular polygon | Size of angle at the centre |
|---|---|---|
| 6 | Regular hexagon | 360° ÷ 6 = 60° |
| 8 | Regular octagon | 360° ÷ 8 = 45° |
| | Regular decagon | |
| | Regular nonagon | |
| | Square | |
| | Equilateral triangle | |

**3** Draw some polygon patterns. Figure 9:9 shows an example. Worksheet 9C can be used to help you.

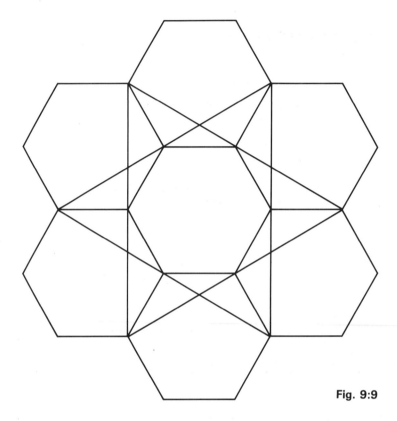

Fig. 9:9

Worksheets 9D to 9H may be used here.

## A Sharing

Division is sharing into equal amounts.

This shows 8 stars shared into 2 equal amounts, giving 4 stars in each part.

We can write this as 8 ÷ 2 = 4.

**1** Write a division statement like 8 ÷ 2 = 4 for the following.

(a)

(b)

(c)

(d)

(e)

(f)

(g)

(h)

**2** There are many ways to say and write what we mean by division.

12 shared into 3 equal parts.

12 ÷ 3

12 divided by 3.

How many 3's in 12?

$\frac{12}{3}$

3)‾12‾

Write all the ways you can think of for 'How many 5s in 20?'

**3** 'What is 24 divided by 6?' is the same as 'How many 6s make 24?'

To do this using the multiplication square you look along row 6 until you find 24. It is in column 4, so 24 ÷ 6 = 4.

| × | 1 | 2 | 3 | 4 | 5 | 6 | 7 | 8 | 9 | 10 |
|---|---|---|---|---|---|---|---|---|---|----|
| 1 | 1 | 2 | 3 | 4 | 5 | 6 | 7 | 8 | 9 | 10 |
| 2 | 2 | 4 | 6 | 8 | 10 | 12 | 14 | 16 | 18 | 20 |
| 3 | 3 | 6 | 9 | 12 | 15 | 18 | 21 | 24 | 27 | 30 |
| 4 | 4 | 8 | 12 | 16 | 20 | 24 | 28 | 32 | 36 | 40 |
| 5 | 5 | 10 | 15 | 20 | 25 | 30 | 35 | 40 | 45 | 50 |
| 6 | 6 | 12 | 18 | 24 | 30 | 36 | 42 | 48 | 54 | 60 |
| 7 | 7 | 14 | 21 | 28 | 35 | 42 | 49 | 56 | 63 | 70 |
| 8 | 8 | 16 | 24 | 32 | 40 | 48 | 56 | 64 | 72 | 80 |
| 9 | 9 | 18 | 27 | 36 | 45 | 54 | 63 | 72 | 81 | 90 |
| 10 | 10 | 20 | 30 | 40 | 50 | 60 | 70 | 80 | 90 | 100 |

Use the multiplication square to answer these questions.

(a)  15 ÷ 3        (b)  24 ÷ 8        (c)  30 ÷ 5        (d)  32 ÷ 4

(e)  24 ÷ 6        (f)  $3\overline{)12}$        (g)  $4\overline{)28}$        (h)  $6\overline{)42}$

(i)  $8\overline{)56}$        (j)  $5\overline{)35}$        (k)  $\dfrac{18}{6}$        (l)  $\dfrac{21}{3}$        (m)  $\dfrac{40}{5}$

(n)  $\dfrac{27}{9}$        (o)  $\dfrac{8}{1}$        (p)  $9\overline{)54}$        (q)  72 ÷ 8

(r)  42 ÷ 7        (s)  $3\overline{)27}$        (t)  63 ÷ 7

**4** Use the multiplication square to find the missing numbers.

(a)  □ ÷ 4 = 5        (b)  □ ÷ 7 = 8        (c)  □ ÷ 8 = 6

(d)  32 ÷ □ = 4        (e)  36 ÷ □ = 9        (f)  □ ÷ 9 = 8

(g)  45 ÷ □ = 5        (h)  64 ÷ □ = 8        (i)  63 ÷ □ = 7

(j)  8 ÷ □ = 8

**5** How many 7s make:

(a) 7    (b) 21    (c) 56    (d) 49    (e) 70?

**6** If the answer to the following questions is 'yes', say how much each.

(a) Can 32 eggs be shared equally among 4 people?

(b) Can 9 girls share 36 sweets equally?

(c)* Is 56 days a whole number of weeks?

(d) Can 8 boys share 72 marbles equally?

(e) Can 9 farmers share 64 sheep equally?

(f) Will 81 plants make 9 equal rows?

(g) Can 52 eggs be packed 6 to a box?

(h) Will 9 go into 63 exactly?

(i) Can you divide 35 by 7 exactly?

(j) Does $\dfrac{54}{6}$ = 9?

# B Sharing with remainder

Figure 10:1 shows a bar of chocolate. If you shared the 10 pieces between 3 people equally, each person will receive 3 blocks but there will be 1 block left over. This block is called the **remainder**.

Fig. 10:1

We can write it like this:

$$\begin{array}{r} 3\ r\ 1 \\ 3\overline{\smash{)}10} \end{array}$$

If you share 11 tennis balls between 4 people equally, each person will have 2 and there will be a remainder of 3.

If you shared 11 apples between 4 people it is possible to share the remainder of 3 apples between them. How? You could not do this with tennis balls. Why not?

The remainder to a division can be written as a fraction:

$$11 \div 4 = 2\ r\ 3 \quad \text{or} \quad 11 \div 4 = 2\tfrac{3}{4}$$

**Note** The remainder 3 becomes $\tfrac{3}{4}$ when we divide it by 4.

- **Remainders on a calculator**

When you use the $\boxed{\div}$ key on a calculator for $12 \div 5$ the display shows $2 \cdot 4$, which is the decimal fraction way to show the remainder $\frac{2}{5}$ or $\frac{4}{10}$.

You can check your answer by multiplying it by 5.

$2 \cdot 4 \times 5 = 12$, which is the amount we started with.

**1**  What is the remainder when:

(a)  15 chocolates are shared equally between 4 people

(b)  20 sweets are shared equally between 3 people

(c)  19 is divided by 6

(d)  $17 \div 5$    (e)  $\dfrac{28}{9}$    (f)  $48 \div 7$    (g)  $36 \div 8$

(h)  42 apples are shared equally between 10 people?

**2 Example**    $13 \div 3 = 4 \text{ r } 1$ or $4\frac{1}{3}$.

Write the remainder in two ways for:

(a)  $15 \div 7$    (b)  $13 \div 5$    (c)  $22 \div 7$    (d)  $20 \div 3$

(e)  $15 \div 4$    (f)  $24 \div 5$    (g)  $11 \div 6$    (h)  $11 \div 8$

(i)  $13 \div 10$

**3**  Use a calculator to find:

(a)  $17 \div 4$    (b)  $19 \div 2$    (c)  $22 \div 5$

(d)  $30 \div 8$    (e)  $12 \div 10$    (f)  $21 \div 4$

(g)  $23 \div 8$    (h)  $38 \div 20$

**4**  In the following say what sign $(+, -, \times$ or $\div)$ should be written instead of the ★.

(a)  Mark has 12p. He gives 8p to Margaret. Mark now has $12 ★ 8$.

(b)  Rashni gives half her 8 japatis to Hassan. She gives Hassan $8 ★ 2$.

(c)  There are 50 buttons in a pack. To buy 100 buttons a manufacturer needs $50 ★ 2$ packs.

(d) Melissa has £24. Toni gives her £14. Melissa now has £24 ★ £14.

(e) Felix owes 3 friends 12 marbles each. He needs 12 ★ 3 marbles.

(f) 4 wheels have 24 spokes altogether. Each wheel is the same. A wheel has 24 ★ 4 spokes.

(g) A class has 32 pupils of which 14 are boys. The number of girls is 32 ★ 14.

(h) 14 scouts eat 42 potatoes. They eat the same number each. One scout eats 42 ★ 14 potatoes.

5 Use your calculator in this question.

(a) 27 saris cost £351. What is the cost of one sari? (They all cost the same amount.)

(b) Share £135 equally among 9 girls.

(c) How many boxes of a dozen eggs can be filled from a container of 1728 eggs?

(d) How many bars of steel 32 mm long can be cut from a long bar of steel, 1120 mm long?

(e) 15 bags of potatoes weigh 55 kg each. What is the total weight?

(f) A video tape can record 360 minutes. It has already recorded 120 minutes. How much is left?

(g) Jenufa is sponsored at £5·68 a length when she swims for the RSPCA. How much does she collect if she swims 15 lengths?

(h) A water-butt contains 75 litres, and my watering can takes 4 litres. How many times can I completely fill it from the butt?

**6** Find the missing numbers in these division calculations.

               7
(a) 6 $\overline{)\; \bigstar\;\; \bigstar}$
            3 r 2
(b) 5 $\overline{)\; \bigstar\;\; \bigstar}$
            9 r 1
(c) 4 $\overline{)\; \bigstar\;\; \bigstar}$

            5 r 2
(d) $\bigstar$ $\overline{)\; 27}$
            $2\frac{2}{3}$
(e) 3 $\overline{)\; \bigstar}$
            $8\frac{3}{5}$
(f) 5 $\overline{)\; \bigstar\;\; \bigstar}$

            $7\frac{1}{4}$
(g) 8 $\overline{)\; \bigstar\;\; \bigstar}$
            $6\;\frac{1}{2}$
(h) 8 $\overline{)\; \bigstar\;\; \bigstar}$
            $3\frac{3}{4}$
(i) $\bigstar$ $\overline{)\; \bigstar\;\; \bigstar}$

            $5\frac{2}{5}$
(j) $\bigstar$ $\overline{)\; \bigstar\;\; \bigstar}$
            $10\frac{1}{10}$
(k) 10 $\overline{)\; \bigstar\;\; \bigstar\;\; \bigstar}$
            $1\frac{1}{4}$
(l) 12 $\overline{)\; \bigstar\;\; \bigstar}$

**7** Write five different division calculations to which the answers are all 4 r 3.

**8** Write five division calculations to which the answers are all $3\frac{2}{3}$.

## ● Coordinates and axes

Figure 11:1 shows a grid.

The **x-axis** is the numbered line that goes across the page.
The **y-axis** is the numbered line that goes up the page.
These two **axes** cross at the **origin**.

'Axes' is the plural of 'axis'.

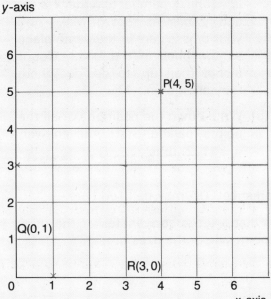

Fig. 11:1

Look at Figure 11:1. If we want to say where point P is on the grid, we start from the origin. The point P is 4 units across and 5 units up. We say it has the coordinates (4, 5).

**Remember** 'Across, then up' or 'x before y'.

The order is important! Can you see why?

## ▶ Points to discuss . . .

1 ▷ Figure 11:2 is a plan which shows the position of some buildings on a housing estate.

The High School is at point (5, 3).

Where are the other buildings? (In other words, what are the coordinates of the other buildings?)

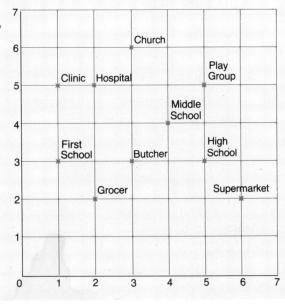

Fig. 11:2

**1 (a)** Copy Figure 11:3 on squared paper (1 cm squares are best for this). Be careful to write the figures on the lines and remember to write 'x-axis' and 'y-axis' as shown. Make sure your crosses are in the same place as the ones in the book. Count along, then up, to decide where they should go.

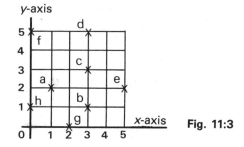

Fig. 11:3

**(b)** Write down the positions of all the points marked. Start your answer:
**a** is (1, 2), **b** is . . .

Worksheet 11A may be used here.

**2** What are the coordinates of the origin (the name of the point where the axes cross)?

**3 (a)** Draw x- and y-axes on squared paper, numbering them from 0 to 5.

**(b)** Plot (mark on the grid) the following points: (2, 5), (3, 4), (3, 3), (2, 2), (2, 1), (2, 0), (1, 0), (1, 1), (1, 2), (0, 3), (0, 4), (1, 5).

**(c)** Check all these points, then use your ruler to join them in the same order as you plotted them.

**4 (a)** Copy Figure 11:4 on squared paper.

**(b)** List the coordinates of every corner, starting at A and going clockwise, like this: (2, 3), (3, 4), etc.

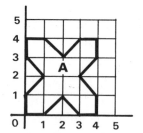

Fig. 11:4

**5 (a)** Draw x- and y-axes on squared paper, numbering them from 0 to 5.

**(b)** Plot the points (2, 4), (3, 3), (3, 1), (2, 0), (1, 0), (0, 1), (0, 3), (1, 4).

**(c)** Use your ruler to join these points in order.

**6** Write down, for Figure 11:5:

(a) the name of the point where line AB
crosses line CD

(b) the coordinates of this point

(c) the name of the line AB

(d) the name of the line CD

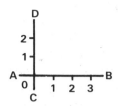

**Fig. 11:5**

Worksheet 11B may be used here.

**7** (a) Draw three pairs of axes on squared paper, numbering them from 0 to 5.

(b) Write the name of each axis at its end.

(c) On one grid plot (1, 0), (1, 3), (3, 3). Join (1, 0) to
(1, 3). Join (1, 3) to (3, 3). Name the coordinates of
a fourth point which, when joined to (3, 3), completes a rectangle.

(d) On the second grid plot (1, 1) and (3, 1). Join them.
Write the coordinates of two points that will make a
square when joined to the first two. Draw the square.

(e) On the third grid join the origin to (1, 2) with a ruler.
Write the coordinates of a third point that will make
an isosceles triangle when joined to the first two, like
Figure 11:6.

Fig. 11:6

**8** (a) Draw a pair of axes, numbered from 0 to 5. Write
their names at their ends.

(b) Plot (1, 1), (3, 1), (3, 3), (1, 3). Join them to make a
square. Then join (3, 1) to (4, 2), (3, 3) to (4, 4), (1, 3)
to (2, 4), (2, 4) to (4, 4), (4, 2) to (4, 4). What is the
name of the solid whose picture you have drawn?

(c) Repeat step (a), then plot the following points,
joining them as necessary to make a picture of a solid
like a matchbox.
(0, 1), (3, 1), (5, 3), (5, 4), (3, 2), (0, 2), (2, 4)

(d) Repeat step (a). Join in order the points (0, 0), (1, 2),
(2, 0), (5, 3), (4, 5), (1, 2). This solid is called an
'isosceles triangular prism'.

A **tessellation** is made up of shapes that join together to cover a surface without leaving any gaps.

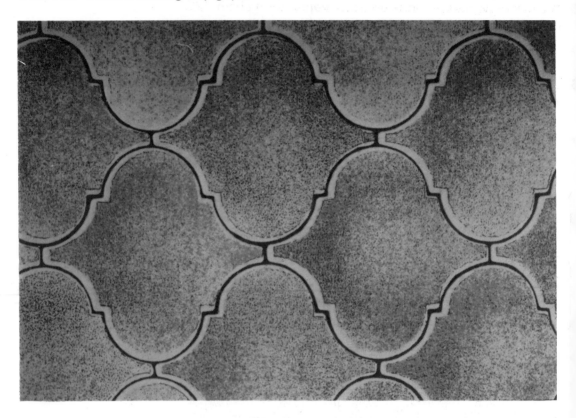

1  You need a set of square tiles. You could cut out your own, or use plastic or card ones supplied by your teacher. The tiles should all be the same size (we say shapes are **congruent** when they are the same shape and size). Will your square tiles tessellate?

2  Will a set of congruent rectangles tessellate?

3  Will a set of congruent triangles tessellate?

4  Sometimes you can use several different shapes together to make a tessellation. Worksheets 12A and 12B have a set of shapes which you can cut out, or your teacher may have some shapes already prepared.

What different tessellations can you make?

If you work in groups you can cut out lots of shapes using coloured paper and make large tessellations for the classroom wall.

5 You can draw tessellations on dotty paper. Worksheet 12C has some ideas to start you off, but feel free to design your own!

6 To find out how to make a tessellation of cat faces you need worksheet 12D.

7 Very interesting patterns can be made by combining patterns on square tiles. Worksheet 12E has some to start you off.

8 Some people get addicted to tessellations. Perhaps you will be one of them! Can you find pictures of some tessellations drawn by the artist M. C. Escher?

## A Measuring area

The **area** of a shape is a measure of the amount of surface it has.

The **perimeter** of a shape is the distance round it.

▶ ## Points to discuss . . .

> 1 What happens when you throw a stone into a still pond?

> 2 What is 'surface'?

> 3 Where does a surface mine-worker work?

> 4 Feel, and describe, different surfaces, such as sand-paper, velvet, polished wood, a file, and a mirror.

> 5 Can we compare the sizes of surfaces by looking at them, or do we have to count or measure?

> 6 How can we measure how much surface something has?

● ## Activities

1 (a) Work with a friend. Compare the surface areas of three large leaves by looking carefully at them.

(b) Arrange the leaves so that the largest is on the left and the smallest is on the right. We call this 'putting the areas in order of size'.

(c) Place the leaves on 5 mm squared paper and draw round them.

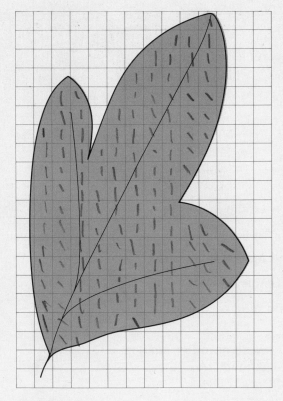

**Fig. 13:1**

(d) Count, and write down, the number of squares each leaf covers. Round the edge, count only those squares where more than half is covered (see Figure 13:2).

 Count this . . .

 not this

**Fig. 13:2**

(e) Was the order you made in (b) correct?

**2** Use 1 cm squared paper to find the area of your hand or your foot. Remember that your results are only approximate (not exact).

The area of your hand is about $\frac{2}{100}$ of the area of your whole skin. This 'hand' measure is used by doctors to describe how much of a person's body has been burned.

**3** Figure 13:3 is a rectangle. It has an area of 12 square centimetres. Each small square is 1 square centimetre (or 1 cm²).

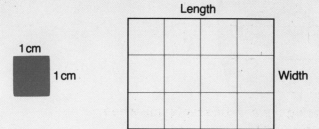

**Fig. 13:3**

(a) What is the length of the rectangle in cm?

(b) What is the width of the rectangle in cm?

(c) What is the perimeter of the rectangle in cm?

(d) What is the area of the rectangle in cm²?

(e) How could you calculate the area of the rectangle from its length and width?

(f) Use 1 cm squared paper. Draw some other shapes with an area of 12 cm². Investigate how the perimeter changes with each different shape.

**1** 'Throaties' sore-throat tablets are packed so that each tablet is in a 1 cm square compartment.
Figure 13:4 shows a Size 1 packet. It is 4 cm long and 2 cm wide.
Size 2 packets are 4 cm long and 3 cm wide.
Size 3 packets are 5 cm long and 4 cm wide.

(a) Draw accurate full-size diagrams of all three packets. Use 1 cm squared paper.

(b) Write under each packet how many tablets it holds, what its area is in cm², and what its perimeter is in cm.

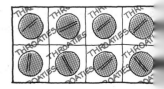

**Fig. 13:**

**2** (a) On 1 cm squared paper draw a rectangle 10 cm long and 4 cm wide.

(b) How many squares of side 1 cm are inside the rectangle?

(c) Write how you worked out your answer to part (b).

**3** (a) On 1 cm squared paper draw three different rectangles (or squares). Copy and complete this table for your rectangles.

| Length | Width | Area |
|--------|-------|------|
|        |       |      |
|        |       |      |
|        |       |      |

(b) Write a rule for calculating the area of a rectangle when you know its length and width.

**4** The area of a rectangle can be calculated using the formula:

$$\text{Area of rectangle} = \text{length} \times \text{width}$$

Both the length and the width must be in the same units, for example, you cannot multiply **4 cm** by **6 metres**.

Calculate the areas of the following in square metres ($m^2$).

(a) A swimming pool 25 metres long and 10 metres wide

(b) A room 3·4 m long and 5·2 m wide

(c) A carpet 2·7 m long and 3·1 m wide

*You may use a calculator.*

Worksheet 13A may be used here.

**5** A square carpet has an area of 16 $m^2$. What is the length of one side of the carpet?

*If you need help, you could draw it on squared paper.*

**6** Copy this table and fill in the missing numbers.

| Rectangle | Length (cm) | Width (cm) | Area (cm²) |
|-----------|-------------|------------|------------|
| Book      | 30          | 20         |            |
| Picture   | 35          | 24         |            |
| Photo     | 15          |            | 150        |
| Envelope  |             | 22         | 660        |

**7** Copy and complete this table for rectangles.

| Length (cm) | Width (cm) | Area (cm²) | Perimeter (cm) |
|:---:|:---:|:---:|:---:|
| 8 | 2 | 16 | 20 |
| 7 | 4 | | |
| 5 | 3 | | |
| 10 | 9 | | |
| 13 | 8 | | |
| 23 | 7 | | |
| 26 | 14 | | |

Worksheet 13C may be used here.

**8** On 1 cm squared paper draw as many rectangles as you can, each with an area of 36 cm². Make a table as in question 7 to record your answers.

**9** On 1 cm squared paper draw as many rectangles as you can, each with a perimeter of 24 cm. Make a table to record your answers.

**10** A farmer has 36 m of fencing. He wishes to make a rectangular sheep pen using the fencing to enclose a grassy area next to another fence. Investigate how he can do this so as to have the largest area possible.

# B Fractional areas

Figure 13:5 is made up from four 1 cm squares and two small rectangles. Each rectangle is half a square, so together they make a whole square. The total area is
4 cm² + 1 cm² = 5 cm².

The same answer can be found by

Area = length × width = 2·5 cm × 2 cm = 5·0 cm².

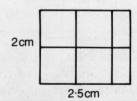

Fig. 13:5

**1** Using 1 cm squared paper draw a rectangle 4·5 cm long and 4 cm wide, then divide it into whole and half squares.

(a) How many whole squares are there in your diagram?

(b) How many half squares are there?

(c) How many cm$^2$ do these whole and half squares make altogether? (Not 20!)

(d) Multiply 4·5 cm by 4 cm and check that your answer agrees with the answer to part (c).

**2** Figure 13:6 has an area of four whole 1 cm squares, four half squares and one quarter square.

Its total area is $6\frac{1}{4}$ cm$^2$ or 6·25 cm$^2$.

This area can be calculated by 2·5 cm × 2·5 cm = 6·25 cm$^2$.

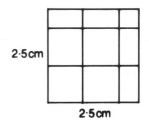

2·5cm

2·5cm

Fig. 13:6

Using 1 cm squared paper, draw a rectangle 3·5 cm long and 1·5 cm wide, then divide it into whole, half and quarter squares.

(a) How many whole squares are there in your diagram?

(b) How many half squares are there?

(c) How many quarter squares are there?

(d) How many cm$^2$ are there altogether?

(e) Check (d) by multiplying 3·5 cm by 1·5 cm.

**3** Yasmin's passport photograph measures 3·5 cm by 5 cm. Calculate its area.

**4** State the areas of the shapes in Figures 13:7. Choose your answers from: 4 cm$^2$; 4·5 cm$^2$; 4·25 cm$^2$.

(a)   (b)   (c)

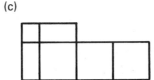

Fig. 13:7

**5** Draw accurately a rectangle 4·5 cm long and 2·5 cm wide. Show by drawing that its area is 11·25 cm$^2$ (eight whole squares, six half squares and one quarter square).

Worksheet 13D may be used here.

## ▶ Points to discuss . . .

Make up a sentence that uses a fraction. Figure 14:1 has some ideas to start you off.

Fig. 14:1

## ● Activities

**1** Fold a piece of paper so that when you open it out the fold lines divide it into two equal parts.
How much of the piece of paper is each of the two parts?

**2** Use a new piece of paper. Fold to divide it into four equal parts.
How much of the piece of paper is each of the four parts?

**3** Now divide pieces of paper into

(a) eight equal pieces    (b) three equal pieces

(c) six equal pieces

# Writing fractions

Figure 14:2 shows shapes divided into four equal parts. We call each part a **quarter** of the shape.

A quarter can be written as $\frac{1}{4}$.

Fig. 14:2

The bottom number tells you into how many equal pieces the whole one has been divided; in $\frac{1}{4}$ it is into 4 pieces.

The top number tells you how many of these equal pieces make up the fraction; in $\frac{1}{4}$ it is 1 piece.

The fraction $\frac{3}{4}$ means divide the whole one into 4 equal pieces (quarters) and take 3 of these pieces (three quarters).

# Common fractions and decimal fractions

When we write a quarter as $\frac{1}{4}$ we call it a **common fraction** (often just called 'a fraction').

When we write a quarter as $0 \cdot 25$ we call it a **decimal fraction** (often just called 'a decimal').

1  In Figure 14:3, what fraction of each shape is shaded? Write each answer in figures and in words.

(a)    (b)    (c)    (d)    (e)

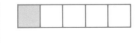
Fig. 14:3

2  Look at Figure 14:4. Tom thinks that a $\frac{1}{4}$ of the rectangle is shaded. Why does he think this? Is he right?

Fig. 14:4

**3 (a)** In Figure 14:5 all the parts of each shape are shaded. Write the shaded part of each shape as a fraction.

**(b)** How many tenths make a whole one?

**4 Example** In Figure 14:6, $\frac{3}{5}$ (three-fifths) is shaded and $\frac{2}{5}$ (two-fifths) is unshaded. $\frac{3}{5} + \frac{2}{5}$ make $\frac{5}{5}$ or a whole one.

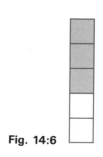

Fig. 14:6

In Figure 14:7, what fraction of each shape is shaded, and what fraction is unshaded? Check that each pair of answers add to make a whole one.

(a)  (b)  (c)  (d)  (e)

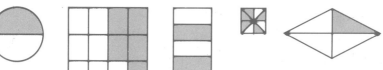

Fig. 14:7

**5 (a)** A quarter of each shape is shaded in Figure 14:8. Are both quarters the same size? Explain what you think 'size' means.

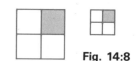

Fig. 14:8

**(b)** Tom and Jerry both have half a brick. Tom's brick is bigger than Jerry's. Either use words, or draw a picture, to show how this is possible.

Worksheets 14A, 14B and 14C may be used here.

**6 Equivalent fractions**

Fig. 14:9

**(a)** Copy Figures 14:9 and 14:10 onto a piece of paper. Cut Figure 14:9 into four quarters and Figure 14:10 into eight eighths.

Fig. 14:10

(b) Use your cut-out pieces to show that $\frac{1}{4}$ of a rectangle is the same size as $\frac{2}{8}$ of the same rectangle.

We say that $\frac{1}{4}$ and $\frac{2}{8}$ are **equivalent fractions**. They are the same amount of a whole one.

**7** Figure 14:11 shows pairs of shapes. Write the pairs of fractions that are shaded. Write = between them if they are equivalent fractions, and ≠ (not equal) if they are not.

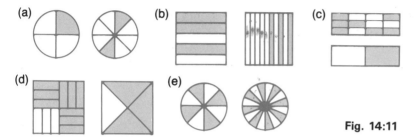

Fig. 14:11

**8** Which of these pairs of common fractions are equivalent?

(a) $\frac{2}{3}$ and $\frac{4}{6}$     (b) $\frac{3}{4}$ and $\frac{9}{12}$     (c) $\frac{2}{5}$ and $\frac{6}{10}$

(d) $\frac{1}{3}$ and $\frac{3}{6}$     (e) $\frac{5}{10}$ and $\frac{1}{2}$     (f) $\frac{7}{10}$ and $\frac{70}{100}$

(g) $\frac{20}{60}$ and $\frac{1}{3}$     (h) $\frac{3}{4}$ and $\frac{6}{10}$

**9** In Figure 14:12, $\frac{5}{12}$ of the dots are enclosed.

Draw six sets of twelve dots, then enclose one of the following fractions of the dots on each of your diagrams:

(a) $\frac{1}{2}$     (b) $\frac{1}{4}$     (c) $\frac{1}{3}$     (d) $\frac{3}{4}$     (e) $\frac{7}{12}$     (f) $\frac{2}{3}$

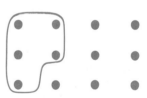

Fig. 14:12

**10** We usually use the simplest form of a fraction. For example, we do not ask for $\frac{2}{4}$ of a cucumber.

When you give fraction answers you should make them as simple as possible by 'cancelling'. Cancelling is dividing the top and bottom numbers by the same number.

Cancelling does not change the value of the fraction. If you *did* ask for $\frac{2}{4}$ of a cucumber you should receive the same amount as if you asked for $\frac{1}{2}$ a cucumber.

**Examples**

$$\frac{8}{12} \xrightarrow[\text{divide by 4}]{\text{divide by 4}} \frac{2}{3}$$

$$\frac{5}{20} \xrightarrow[\text{divide by 5}]{\text{divide by 5}} \frac{1}{4}$$

Find in its simplest form the fraction of each of the drawings in Figure 14:13 that is shaded. Show how you worked your answer out, and write it in both figures and words.

(a)  (b)  (c)  (d)  (e)

(f)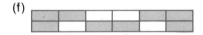

**Fig. 14:13**

11 Look at Figure 14:14. It shows that $\frac{1}{4}$ is the same fraction of the large square as $\frac{4}{16}$.

We say that $\frac{1}{4}$ and $\frac{4}{16}$ are equivalent fractions.

**Fig. 14:14**

Multiplying both numbers in a fraction by the same number does not change the value of the fraction.

Dividing both numbers in a fraction by the same number does not change the value of the fraction.

(a) Which of the following fractions are equivalent to $\frac{1}{2}$?
$$\frac{2}{4}, \ \frac{4}{10}, \ \frac{2}{8}, \ \frac{6}{12}, \ \frac{8}{16}, \ \frac{2}{20}, \ \frac{5}{10}$$

(b) Which of the following fractions are the same as $\frac{1}{4}$?
$$\frac{2}{4}, \ \frac{2}{8}, \ \frac{3}{6}, \ \frac{3}{12}, \ \frac{4}{10}, \ \frac{4}{12}, \ \frac{4}{16}, \ \frac{5}{20}$$

(c) Which of the following fractions are equivalent to $\frac{1}{3}$?
$$\frac{2}{4}, \ \frac{2}{6}, \ \frac{3}{6}, \ \frac{3}{9}, \ \frac{5}{10}, \ \frac{4}{10}, \ \frac{4}{12}, \ \frac{5}{15}, \ \frac{10}{30}$$

(d) Which of the following fractions are equal to $\frac{3}{4}$?
$$\frac{2}{4}, \ \frac{6}{8}, \ \frac{3}{6}, \ \frac{3}{12}, \ \frac{4}{10}, \ \frac{9}{12}, \ \frac{4}{16}, \ \frac{15}{20}$$

(e) Which of the following fractions are the same as $\frac{2}{5}$?
$$\frac{1}{5}, \ \frac{4}{10}, \ \frac{5}{15}, \ \frac{8}{20}, \ \frac{10}{30}, \ \frac{12}{30}, \ \frac{20}{50}, \ \frac{6}{15}$$

12 Copy and complete:

(a) $\frac{1}{2} = \frac{2}{4} = \frac{\star}{6} = \frac{\star}{8} = \frac{\star}{10} = \frac{6}{\star} = \frac{7}{\star} = \frac{8}{\star}$

(b) $\frac{1}{3} = \frac{2}{6} = \frac{3}{9} = \frac{\star}{12} = \frac{\star}{15} = \frac{6}{\star} = \frac{7}{\star} = \frac{8}{\star}$

(c) $\frac{1}{4} = \frac{2}{8} = \frac{3}{12} = \frac{\star}{20} = \frac{8}{\star} = \frac{11}{\star} = \frac{12}{\star} = \frac{\star}{100}$

**13** $\frac{1}{2}$, $\frac{1}{3}$, $\frac{1}{4}$, $\frac{4}{8}$, $\frac{6}{12}$, $\frac{3}{12}$, $\frac{4}{16}$, $\frac{8}{16}$, $\frac{5}{10}$, $\frac{3}{9}$, $\frac{5}{20}$, $\frac{4}{12}$, $\frac{5}{15}$

(a) Copy these fractions. Put a ring round each one that is the same as a half.

(b) Copy the fractions again. Put a ring round each one that is the same as a third.

(c) Copy the fractions again. Put a ring round the ones equal to a quarter.

**14** Copy the following, replacing the stars with numbers to make the pairs of fractions equivalent.

(a) $\frac{1}{4} = \frac{\star}{12}$    (b) $\frac{2}{6} = \frac{\star}{3}$    (c) $\frac{1}{5} = \frac{2}{\star}$    (d) $\frac{8}{10} = \frac{4}{\star}$

(e) $\frac{5}{6} = \frac{\star}{12}$    (f) $\frac{3}{8} = \frac{\star}{24}$    (g) $\frac{20}{30} = \frac{2}{\star}$    (h) $\frac{9}{15} = \frac{\star}{5}$

(i) $\frac{100}{400} = \frac{\star}{4}$    (j) $\frac{5}{8} = \frac{50}{\star}$

**15** In Figure 14:15, $2\frac{1}{2}$ (two and a half) squares have been shaded.

How many squares are shaded in each part of Figure 14:16?

Fig. 14:15

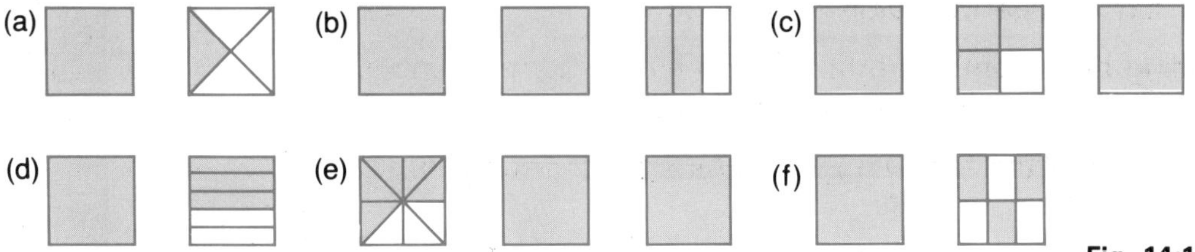

(a)    (b)    (c)

(d)    (e)    (f)

Fig. 14:16

**16** A fraction like $\frac{7}{4}$ is called a **top-heavy fraction**, or 'improper' fraction.

A number like $1\frac{3}{4}$ is called a **mixed number**.

Example    $\frac{17}{4}$ will make 4 whole ones (16 quarters) with one quarter left over, so $\frac{17}{4} = 4\frac{1}{4}$.

Change the following top-heavy fractions to mixed numbers.

(a) $\frac{5}{4}$    (b) $\frac{15}{4}$    (c) $\frac{9}{8}$    (d) $\frac{11}{8}$    (e) $\frac{7}{6}$    (f) $\frac{9}{5}$

(g) $\frac{11}{7}$    (h) $\frac{30}{7}$

**17 Example**  $1\frac{3}{4}$ is one whole plus $\frac{3}{4}$.
We can write this as $\frac{4}{4} + \frac{3}{4} = \frac{7}{4}$.

The mixed number $1\frac{3}{4}$ is equivalent to the top-heavy fraction $\frac{7}{4}$.

**Example**  $2\frac{2}{5}$ is two wholes plus $\frac{2}{5}$.

We can write this as $\frac{5}{5} + \frac{5}{5} + \frac{2}{5} = \frac{12}{5}$.

The mixed number $2\frac{2}{5}$ is equivalent to the top-heavy (or 'improper') fraction $\frac{12}{5}$.

Change the following mixed numbers into top-heavy fractions.

(a) $1\frac{2}{3}$    (b) $1\frac{1}{4}$    (c) $1\frac{3}{5}$    (d) $2\frac{3}{4}$    (e) $2\frac{1}{5}$

(f) $2\frac{1}{10}$    (g) $3\frac{1}{3}$    (h) $3\frac{3}{4}$

**18 Example**  Figure 14:17 shows part of an inch ruler.
Each inch is divided into 4 parts.
The distance between the arrows is $1\frac{3}{4}$ inches.

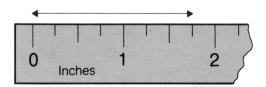

Fig. 14:17

**Example**  Figure 14:18 shows part of another inch ruler.
Each inch is now divided into 8 parts.
The distance between the arrows is $1\frac{5}{8}$ inches.

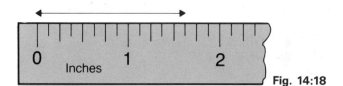

Fig. 14:18

Write the distances from the zero mark (Z) to each of the letters A to I on the ruler in Figure 14:19.

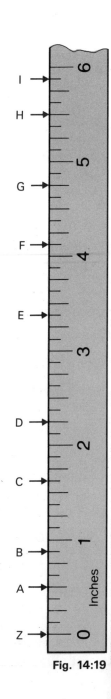

Fig. 14:19

**19** Figure 14:20 shows some gauge readings. The reading is made by looking at the right-hand end of the thick line. Write the readings for each gauge, both as a mixed number and as top-heavy fraction.

(a)

(b)

(c)

(d)

Fig. 14:20

**20** Give the reading on each dial in Figure 14:21, both as a mixed number and as a top-heavy fraction, as simply as possible.

Fig. 14:21

(a)

(b)
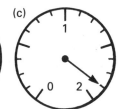

(c)
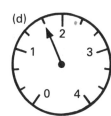

(d)
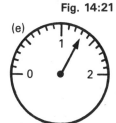

(e)

**21** Figure 14:22 shows a series of fractions called a **Farey sequence**. Find the line labelled $\frac{1}{3}$. It goes through the point (3, 1), giving $\frac{1}{3}$. The line labelled 2 goes through (1, 2), giving $\frac{2}{1} = 2$.

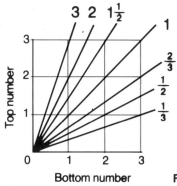

(a) Copy the diagram. Check the fractions.

(b) The steeper the slope of a line, the bigger the fraction, so:
$3 > 2 > 1\frac{1}{2} > 1 > \frac{2}{3} > \frac{1}{2} > \frac{1}{3}$

Draw a grid 0 to 4 and draw labelled lines as in Figure 14:22 to show whole numbers and fractions from 4 to $\frac{1}{4}$. Then write them in order using the > sign.

**22** Try question 21 for bigger grids. Try to find out more about Farey sequences.

# A Metric weight

## ● Metric units of weight

**gram (g)**      About the same as two drawing pins
**kilogram (kg)**   A 'standard' bag of sugar
**tonne (tonne)**   A Mini-Metro weighs about $\frac{3}{4}$ of a tonne

$$1000 \text{ g} = 1 \text{ kg}$$
$$1000 \text{ kg} = 1 \text{ tonne}$$

## ▶ Points to discuss . . .

1. What could you weigh on the weighing machines in Figures 15:1, 15:2 and 15:3?

2. How many different weighing machines can you think of?
Perhaps you could put some on display in your classroom.

Fig. 15:1

Fig. 15:2

Fig. 15:3

**1** (a) List the objects in Figure 15:4, one under the other in order of weight, heaviest first.

Fig. 15:4

(b) After each object in your list write its weight, chosen from: 13 g, 10 tonnes, $\frac{1}{2}$ g, 1 kg, 80 000 tonnes, 100 g, 25 kg.

**2** How many grams make:

(a) 1 kg　　(b) 5 kg　　(c) $\frac{1}{2}$ kg　　(d) $\frac{1}{4}$ kg?

**3** Figure 15:5 shows a weighing scale which gives readings in kilograms and in grams. The pointer shows the reading 1·5 kg or 1500 g.

Give the readings on the scales in Figure 15:6 both in kg and in g, as in the example.

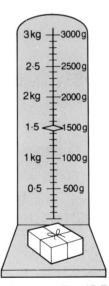

Fig. 15:5

(a) 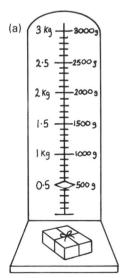　　(b) 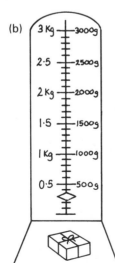　　(c)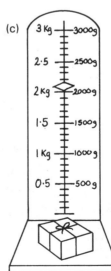

Fig. 15.6

The diagram on the right will help you to answer questions 4 and 5.

4  How many grams make:

(a)  1·5 kg     (b)  1·7 kg     (c)  2·1 kg     (d)  3·6 kg

(e)  0·5 kg     (f)  .0·1 kg     (g)  0·2 kg     (h)  0·9 kg?

5  Write in kg:

(a)  3000 g     (b)  2500 g     (c)  2100 g     (d)  100 g

(e)  800 g     (f)  400 g

6  How could you use a calculator:

(a)  to convert from kilograms to grams

(b)  to convert from grams to kilograms?

THINK!
If we use smaller units, we will have more.

7  Your answer to question 6 should say something like:

(a)  multiply by 1000     (b)  divide by 1000

Copy and complete the following. You may use a calculator if you wish.

(a)  1·5 kg = . . . g     (b)  1·50 kg = . . . g

(c)  1·500 kg = . . . g     (d)  0·5 kg = . . . g

(e)  0·50 kg = . . . g     (f)  0·500 kg = . . . g

(g)  2 kg = . . . g     (h)  20 kg = . . . g

(i)  200 kg = . . . g

8  Copy and complete:

(a)  2650 g = . . . kg     (b)  1002 g = . . . kg

(c)  1856 g = . . . kg     (d)  856 g = . . . kg

(e)  56 g = . . . kg     (f)  6 g = . . . kg

**9** Copy the following sentences, completing them with a weight chosen from:

7 g, 250 g, 1 kg, 45 kg, 0·5 tonne.

(a) Tina is 12 years old. She weighs . . .

(b) A bag of sugar weighs . . .

(c) A 2p coin weighs . . .

(d) A packet of butter weighs . . .

(e) Cy's car weighs . . .

**10** Write ten weights in grams and ten weights in kilograms. Change books with a classmate and see which of you can change the units (g to kg and kg to g) the faster.

**11**

| Postal rates – overseas Letters and postcards | | | | | | | |
|---|---|---|---|---|---|---|---|
| Not over | £  p | Not over | £  p | Not over | £  p |
| 20 g | 22 | 300 g | 1 25 | 1000 g | 3 52 |
| 60 g | 37 | 350 g | 1 44 | 1250 g | 4 07 |
| 100 g | 53 | 400 g | 1 64 | 1500 g | 4 62 |
| 150 g | 70 | 450 g | 1 83 | 1750 g | 5 17 |
| 200 g | 88 | 500 g | 2 02 | 2000 g | 5 72 |
| 250 g | 1 06 | 750 g | 2 77 | | |

This table shows the postal rates for overseas mail in 1987. You may prefer to use an up-to-date table for these questions.

State the cost of sending the following weights at the overseas letters rate.

(a)  18 g      (b)  65 g      (c)  360 g      (d)  1·1 kg

(e)  1·45 kg      (f)  250 g      (g)  255 g      (h)  425 g

(i)  2 kg      (j)  1600 g

**12 (a)** Sally weighed this letter on the letter balance. What will it cost her to send it overseas?

Fig. 15:7

Look back at the table on page 115.

**(b)** This letter has been weighed and is ready for posting overseas.

Fig. 15:8

What do you think it weighed? Is there more than one possible answer?

**13** Match the games balls to their approximate weights.

**Weights**   2·5 g,   160 g,   400 g,   420 g,   24 g,   46 g,   57 g

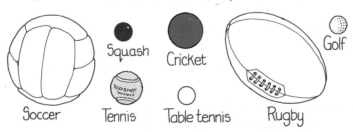

Soccer    Squash    Cricket    Tennis    Table tennis    Rugby    Golf

Fig. 15:9

# B Arithmetic in metric weight

As long ago as 1938 doctors kept alive a baby girl called Marion who was only 31 cm long and weighed only 283 g at birth. Hers is probably the lowest recorded birth weight for a surviving infant.

The average weight for a normal baby girl is about 2·95 kg. About how many times heavier than Marion is this?

Perhaps you could make two dolls to represent the two babies. You could use bottles for the bodies, filling them with sand to make the right weights. Compare the feel of the different weights.

## ▶ Points to discuss . . .

1▷ Which of the parcels in Figure 15:10 can be put together to weigh:

(a) about a kilogram    (b) about ½ a kilogram

(c) about 2 kilograms?

Fig. 15:10

1 Ivan is adding 0·5 kg weights to his scales. What will be the next four readings if he begins with the scales reading:

(a) 2·1 kg    (b) 2·4 kg    (c) 3·3 kg    (d) 2·7 kg?

2 Connie is adding 0·1 kg weights to her scales. What will the next four readings after:

(a) 4·8 kg    (b) 3·6 kg    (c) 5·7 kg    (d) 1·9 kg?

3 Abraham has some sand on his scales. He removes 0·1 kg at a time. What will be the next four readings when he starts with the following weights of sand:

(a) 5·3 kg    (b) 3·1 kg    (c) 6·0 kg    (d) 4·0 kg?

**4** On a day's fishing trip, Jake caught a big dab and Jean caught a small plaice. Write down the weight of each fish.

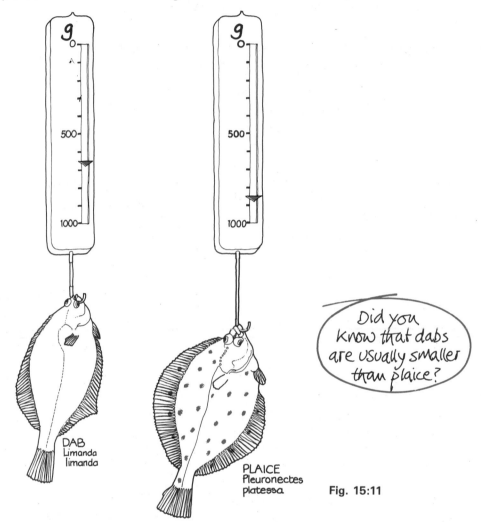

Fig. 15:11

Did you know that dabs are usually smaller than plaice?

DAB
Limanda
limanda

PLAICE
Pleuronectes
platessa

Find the difference in weight between the two fishes.

**5** On Sundays Hannah does a paper round: She delivers the *Sunday Times* to 15 houses. One Sunday she weighs one *Sunday Times*, as shown in Figure 15:12. What total weight of *Sunday Times* did she deliver that day?

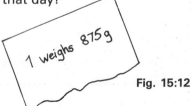

1 weighs 875 g

Fig. 15:12

**6** Nathan adds 1·5 kg and 750 g and makes the answer 751·5 kg. He realises this cannot be right. Why is it obviously wrong? What mistake has he made?

**7** When adding mixed weights you may find it easier to change all the kg to g, add up, then change the answer back to kg.

**Example**   450 g + 1·75 kg + 0·02 kg
= 450 g + 1750 g + 20 g
= 2220 g
= 2·220 kg (or just 2·22 kg)

Try these.
(a)  1 kg 400 g + 360 g + 208 g
(b)  2 kg + 1·8 kg + 2·7 kg
(c)  0·94 kg + 3·6 kg
(d)  900 g + 450 g + 3 kg + 1·5 kg
(e)  3 kg − 600 g
(f)  4 kg − 1·6 kg

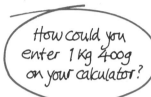

How could you enter 1 Kg 400g on your calculator?

1400
360
208
‾‾‾‾
1968

**8** The answer to a question about weights in kilograms was shown as 1·005 on a calculator display. What weight is this in kilograms and grams?

1.005

**9** Hassan looked at these old scales. Most of the weights were missing. Only the 20 g, the 50 g and the 200 g weights were still there. What quantities of rice could he weigh?

**10** Are you sure you found all the possible weights in question 9? Have another think about it.

Fig. 15:13

**11** Write about how you could find the weight of one Smartie using the things in Figure 15:14.

Fig. 15:14

# C Capacity

The **capacity** of a container is a measure of the amount of space inside it.

> ▶ ## Points to discuss . . .

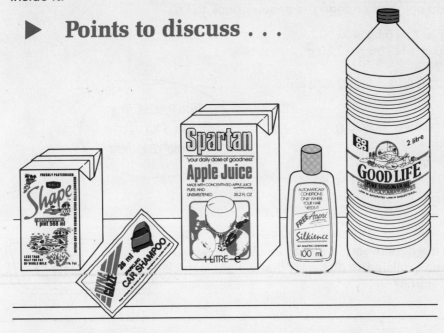

Fig. 15:15

When measuring capacity, two of the units most often used are
   the litre,
   the millilitre.
1000 ml = 1 litre.

In the British Isles, milk is usually still sold by the pint. (1989)
Another unit sometimes used is the centilitre.
100 centilitres = 1000 millilitres = 1 litre

**1**   1 litre,   4 ml,   200 ml,   5 litres

Which of the above capacities belongs to each object in Figure 15:16?

Fig. 15:16

**2 Example**  The measuring container in Figure 15:17 gives readings in both millilitres and litres. It now contains 400 ml or 0·4 litres.

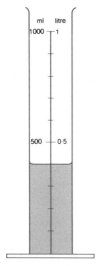

**Fig. 15:17**

How much liquid is in each of the containers in Figure 15:18?
Give your answer both in ml and in litres.

(a) 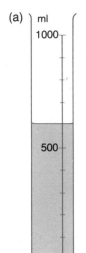 (b) 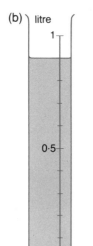 (c) 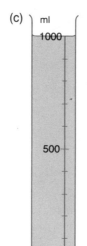 (d)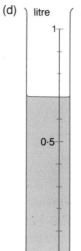

**Fig. 15:18**

**3** (a) Write these in litres:  500 ml,  200 ml,  800 ml.

(b) Write these in millilitres:  0·1 litre,  0·5 litre,  0·3 litre,  1 litre.

**4** How could you use a calculator to convert:

(a) from litres to millilitres

(b) from millilitres to litres?

**5** Your answer to question 4 should be something like:

(a) multiply by 1000    (b) divide by 1000.

Use your calculator to change:

(a) $1\frac{1}{2}$ litres to ml    (b) $0 \cdot 1$ litres to ml

(c) $0 \cdot 01$ litres to ml    (d) $0 \cdot 001$ litres to ml

**6** Use your calculator to change:

(a) 2000 ml to litres    (b) 200 ml to litres

(c) 20 ml to litres    (d) 2 ml to litres

**7** Write some rules to help a friend convert between litres, centilitres, and millilitres.

**8** Kalinda made a model water lift. She found that 500 ml of water was just enough to raise it. About what weight do you think the cabin is?

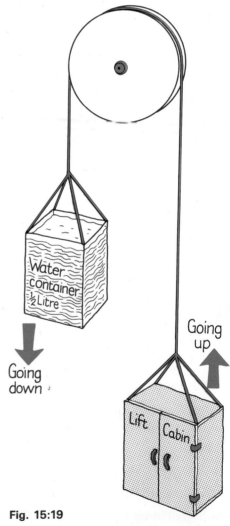

Fig. 15:19

**9** Janet wondered how many times she could clean her hands using the new soap dispenser. She found that three pushes filled a 5 ml medicine spoon. What answer do you think Janet came up with?

Fig. 15:20

**10** The tap in Ben's bathroom drips. He put a beaker underneath for 10 minutes and collected 88 ml of water.

Roughly how much water will be wasted in

(a) an hour    (b) a day    (c) a month    (d) a year?

528 mL

---

**11** How many buckets of water is your answer to question 10 part (d)? How big is a bucket? That's your problem!

**12** Imagine that you have to talk to a group of children about imperial and metric measures. What measurements will you tell them about? How interesting can you make it? What examples will you use? What objects will you take with you? Maybe a local primary school would be interested to let you come to talk to one of their classes.

# Project: reflection in a mirror

**1** (a) When you look in a mirror and hold up your right arm, which arm does your reflection hold up?

(b) Find out why a mirror seems to reverse right to left but not top to bottom.

**2** 'Just look at yourself!' said Marmaduke's mum, holding up her mirror. Figure 16:1 shows what Marmaduke saw. Draw what his mother saw. Be very careful with the eyes, ears, hair, nose, mouth and tie. Check your answer with a mirror.

Fig. 16:1

**3** Write the words shown in Figure 16:2 as they would appear when reflected in a mirror.

# HAM SPAM EGGS BEANS
Fig. 16:2

**4** Write a short sentence that can be read in a mirror, like the one in Figure 16:3.

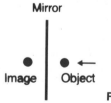

Fig. 16:3

**5** In questions 1 to 4 you have been looking into the mirror. Now you are going to look down onto the mirror's edge and pretend you can see both the object (the real thing) and the image (the reflection in the mirror).

The mirror will be represented by a line.

Look at Figure 16:4. Turn your book and look in the direction of the arrow, then slowly slide a mirror along the mirror line. Check that the image is where it has been drawn.

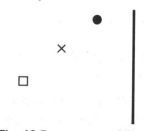

Fig. 16:4

**6** Jane is 1 metre from a mirror. How far from Jane is her image?

**7** Copy Figure 16:5 exactly, leaving a 4 cm space to the right of the mirror line. Draw the images of the three objects. Check your answer with a mirror.

Fig. 16:5          Mirror

**8** Copy Figure 16:6 exactly, leaving a 4 cm space below and to the right of the mirror lines. Draw the images in each mirror.

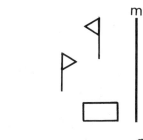

— m    **Fig. 16:6**

**9** Copy and continue Figure 16:7 for all the capital letters of the alphabet.

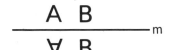

— m    **Fig. 16:7**

**10** Only one of the diagrams in Figure 16:8 is correct. What is wrong with the other three?

(a)  m        (b) m        (c)        (d)

    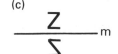  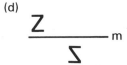

**Fig. 16:8**

**11** Copy Figure 16:9 exactly. Reflect the ● and the **X**, measuring carefully, then join each object to its image with a straight line.

**12** Copy Figure 16:10 exactly. Reflect the flag in the mirror. (It is best to reflect each end first, then join the ends with a line.)

**Fig. 16:9**

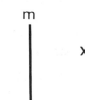

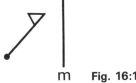

m    **Fig. 16:10**

**13** (a) Copy Figure 16:11 exactly, then reflect the objects in the mirror.

(b) Join the objects together and the images together to make a triangle and its reflection.

**Fig. 16:11**

**14** Place a mirror in line with the arrows on Figure 16:12, then turn it through 360°, keeping it on the centre dot.

Repeat for Figure 16:13, then draw some of your own.

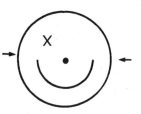

Fig. 16:12

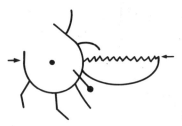

Fig. 16:13

**15** In a kaleidoscope, mirrors give reflections to make a pattern, like the one in Figure 16:14. Draw and colour a kaleidoscope pattern.

Fig. 16:14

**16** Stand two mirrors on edge as shown in Figure 16:15. They must be exactly at right-angles. Comment on your reflection in the mirrors. Repeat the experiment with one mirror horizontal and one vertical.

Fig. 16:15

# 17  Reflection on a grid

In Figure 17:1, A' is the **image** of A.

The image of a point is always the same distance behind the mirror as the object point is in front.

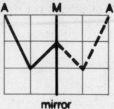

**Example** In Figure 17:1, AM = A'M.

Fig. 17:1

The line joining an object point to an image point always crosses the mirror line at 90°.

**Example** In Figure 17:1, the line joining A to A' crosses the mirror line at 90°.

**1** Copy Figure 17:2 on squared paper, then draw the images in the mirrors.

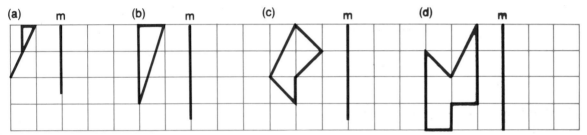

Fig. 17:2

**2** Copy Figure 17:3, then draw in the positions of the mirrors.

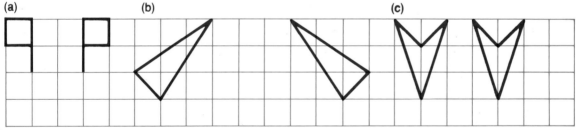

Fig. 17:3

**3** Copy Figure 17:4 on squared paper, then draw the images in the mirrors.

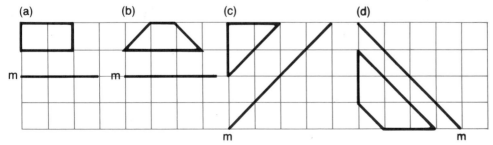

Fig. 17:4

**4** Copy Figure 17:5 on squared paper, then draw the images in the mirrors.

(a)  (b)

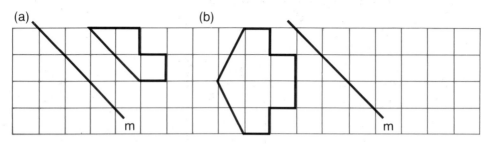

Fig. 17:5

**5** Copy Figure 17:6 on squared paper, then draw in possible mirror lines. If you can see two possible lines, draw them both.

(a)  (b)  (c)  (d)

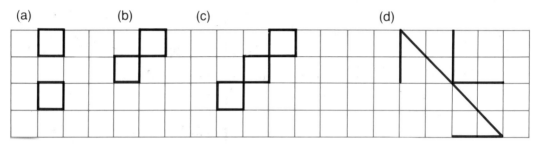

Fig. 17:6

**6** (a)  Copy Figure 17:7 and draw the images.
(A′ is the image of A.)

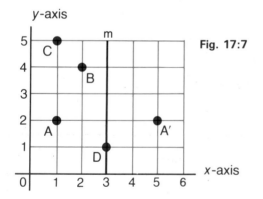

Fig. 17:7

(b)  Copy and complete the table.

|  | Coordinates | |
|---|---|---|
| Object letter | Object | Image |
| A | (1, 2) | (5, 2) |
| B |  |  |
| C |  |  |
| D |  |  |

**7** (a)  Figure 17:8 shows an object, A, reflected twice in a mirror m. The first image's position is marked A′ and the second is marked A″. Copy Figure 17:8 and mark the images B′, B″, C′ and C″.

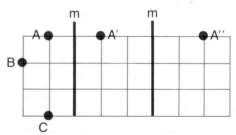

Fig. 17:8

(b) Join ABC and A′B′C′ and A″B″C″ to make 3 triangles.

(c) Comment on the second reflection of triangle ABC.

**8** Copy Figure 17:9. Draw the first and second reflection of the pentagon.

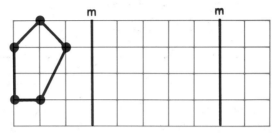

Fig. 17:9

**9** (a) Copy Figure 17:10 and mark the images B′, C′ and D′.

(b) Join ABCD and A′B′C′D′.

(c) Draw up and complete a table like the one in question 6 (b).

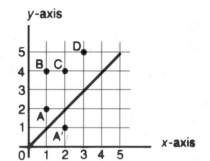

Fig. 17:10

**0** (a) Copy the axes and the mirror line, but not the points, shown in Figure 17:10.

(b) Plot (3, 3), (1, 3), (2, 4) and (2, 5). Join them in order, making a four-sided figure (a concave quadrilateral).

(c) Reflect the figure in the mirror and state the co-ordinates of the image.

Fig. 17:11

Worksheet 17 may be used here.

**11** Copy Figure 17:11 and reflect the objects in all four mirror lines. Think very carefully about the hatched shading lines.

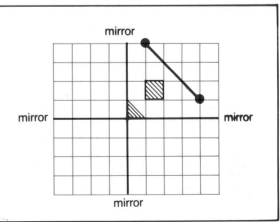

# Symmetry: line

1> What is meant by symmetry?

2> What symmetrical objects can you see from where you are now?

3> Make a classroom collection of objects that have symmetry.

**1** Figure 18:1 shows a folded sheet of paper. Draw the shape you would see if you cut along the two sloping lines and opened out the piece you had cut out. Use a pair of scissors to check your answer.

Experiment with other cut-outs. Each time draw what you expect to see when you open out the cut-out, **before** you do any cutting.

You could make more than one fold if you want to make this more challenging.

Worksheet 18A may be used here.

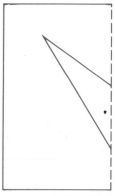

**Fig. 18:1**

**2** Copy Figure 18:2. Mark each picture's lines of symmetry, or write 'It has none'.

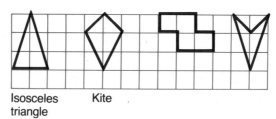

Isosceles triangle    Kite

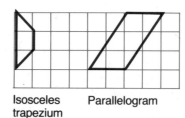

Isosceles trapezium    Parallelogram

**Fig. 18:2**

**3** The rectangle in Figure 18:3 has two
lines of symmetry. Copy Figure 18:4 and
mark in the lines of symmetry.

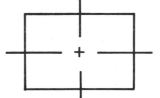

Fig. 18:3

 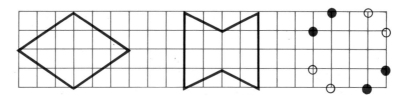

Fig. 18:4

Worksheet 18B may be used here.

**4** In your book, draw all the capital letters, making them
three spaces high. Mark all the lines of symmetry (though
you need not do **all** of them on the letter O).

**5** Draw four circles, the same diameter as your protractor.
Mark the points shown in Figure 18:5. Join the following
sets of points, one set on each diagram.

(a) 0°–120°–240°–0°;
an equilateral triangle

(b) 0°–90°–180°–270°–0°;
a square

(c) 0°–60°–120°–180°–240°–
300°–0°; a regular hexagon

(d) 0°–45°–90°–135°–225°–
270°–315°–0°;
a regular octagon

Worksheets 18C to 18E may be used here.

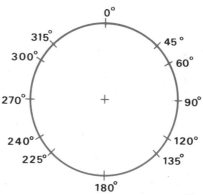

Fig. 18:5

# 9 Triangles: types; angle sum

## A Kinds of triangle

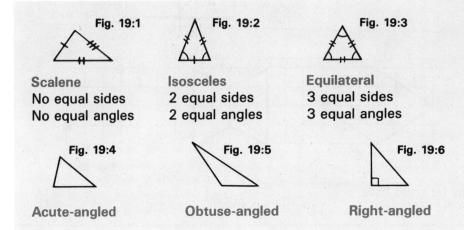

Fig. 19:1

Scalene
No equal sides
No equal angles

Fig. 19:2

Isosceles
2 equal sides
2 equal angles

Fig. 19:3

Equilateral
3 equal sides
3 equal angles

Fig. 19:4

Acute-angled

Fig. 19:5

Obtuse-angled

Fig. 19:6

Right-angled

### Activities

**1** Figure 19:7 shows how to fold an equilateral triangle.

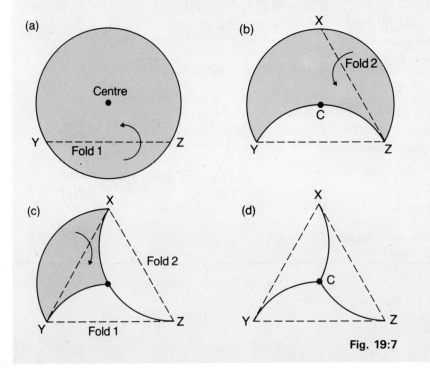

(a)
Centre
Fold 1
Y
Z
(b)
X
Fold 2
C
Y
Z
(c)
X
Fold 2
Y
Fold 1
Z
(d)
X
C
Y
Z


Fig. 19:7

**2** Figure 19:8 shows how to fold a right-angled triangle.

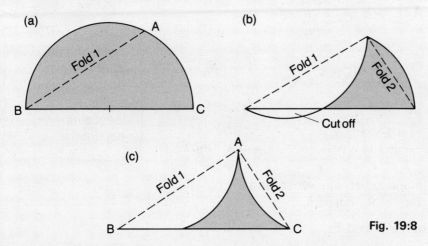

(a) (b) (c)

Fold 1, Fold 2, Cut off

B, A, C

**Fig. 19:8**

Does it matter how far round the arc you make point A?

**1** Fold a rectangle of paper and cut off a corner, as shown in Figure 19:9. **Wait!** First write down what sort of triangle you think you will have cut out. Then see if you are right!

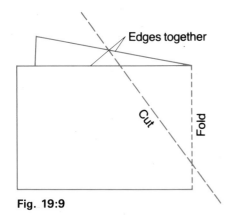

Edges together

Cut

Fold

**Fig. 19:9**

**2** Repeat question 1 for Figure 19:10.

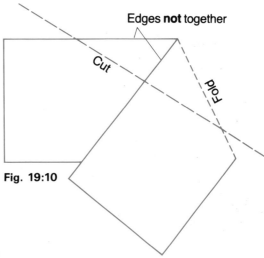

Edges **not** together

Cut

Fold

**Fig. 19:10**

Worksheets 19A and 19B may be used here.

**3** Copy Figure 19:11. C is the centre of the semi-circle. P is any
point on the arc.

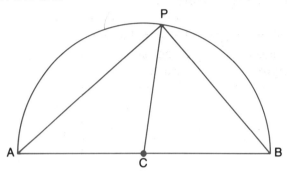

Fig. 19:11

right-angled
acute-angled
obtuse-angled
scalene
isosceles
equilateral

Using words from the above list, say what kind of triangle
has the following letters at its corners.

(a) A, P and B     (b) A, C and P     (c) C, P and B

**4** Which of the triangles in Figure 19:12 is:

(a) equilateral     (b) isosceles right-angled

(c) isosceles obtuse-angled     (d) scalene obtuse-angled

(e) isosceles acute-angled?

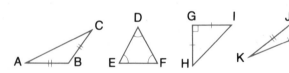 

Fig. 19:12

**5** (a) Use a protractor and a ruler to draw an isosceles
triangle, an equilateral triangle, and a scalene triangle.

(b) On each triangle draw in all its lines of symmetry.

**6** Copy these sentences, completing them with 'All',
'Some', or 'No'.

(a) . . . equilateral triangles are isosceles triangles.

(b) . . . right-angled triangles are equilateral triangles.

(c) . . . isosceles triangles are right-angled triangles.

(d) . . . right-angled triangles are obtuse-angled.

(e) . . . acute-angled triangles are isosceles triangles.

**7** Copy the table. Where possible, draw a triangle in each space. If it is not possible, draw a spider instead.

|  | All sides are of different lengths | Two sides are of equal length | Three sides are of equal length |
|---|---|---|---|
| Acute-angled |  |  |  |
| Right-angled |  |  |  |
| Obtuse-angled |  |  |  |

**8** Use your protractor and a ruler to draw an equilateral triangle of side 10 cm.

Place a dot anywhere within the triangle. Measure the distance from the dot to each side of the triangle – choose the shortest distance each time.

Make a table which shows your results.

Investigate what happens to the lengths for different positions of the dot in the triangle.

# B Angle sum of a triangle

● **Activities**

**1** On a sheet of lined paper draw a large triangle. Cut out your triangle.

Now make three folds as shown in Figures 19:13 and 19:14. The three angles of the triangle have come together to make a straight line.

How many degrees is the sum of the three angles of a triangle?

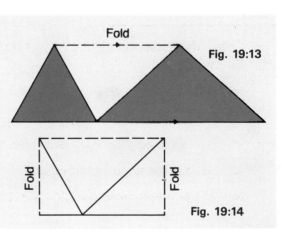

Fold

Fig. 19:13

Fold    Fold

Fig. 19:14

**2** Cut out another triangle. Tear off the three corners. Do they make a straight line when they are put together? What does an angle of 180° look like?

**The angles of a triangle add up to 180°.**

**1 Example** Find the size of angle *a* in Figure 19:15.

Add the two known angles:

$$\begin{array}{r} 59° \\ + 37° \\ \hline 96° \end{array}$$

Subtract the total from 180° to find the size of the third angle *a*.

$$\begin{array}{r} 180° \\ - 96° \\ \hline 84° \end{array}$$

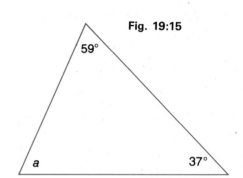

Fig. 19:15

Calculate the sizes of the lettered angles in Figure 19:16. Set out your working as in the example. (Do not try to measure the angles. They are not drawn the correct size.)

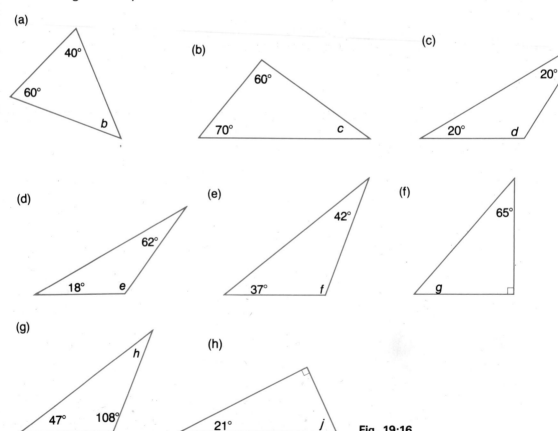

Fig. 19:16

**2** An isosceles triangle has one line of symmetry (see Figure 19:17).

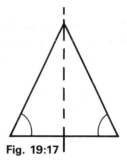

Fig. 19:17

(a) What must be true about the two angles marked with an arc?

(b) One angle of an isosceles triangle is 70°. Find two possible pairs of answers for the other two angles.

(c) What could the angles be in a right-angled isosceles triangle?

**3** State all three angles of a triangle that is:

(a) right-angled with one angle 23°

(b) right-angled with two equal angles

(c) isosceles with one angle 100°

(d) isosceles with one angle 60°

(e) isosceles with one angle 72° (two possible answers)

**4** Can an obtuse-angled isosceles triangle have an angle of 46°? If so, state the sizes of the other two angles.

Worksheet 19C may be used here.

# A What is a percentage?

In Figure 20:1, 23 out of the 100 squares have been shaded.

This could be written as a fraction:
$\frac{23}{100}$ of the diagram.

It could also be written as a percentage:
23% of the diagram.

The % sign is read as 'per cent'.

Fig. 20:1

1 Write as a fraction and as a percentage the amount shaded in each part of Figure 20:2.

(a)
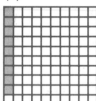

(b)
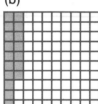

(c)
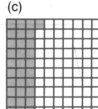

(d) (e)
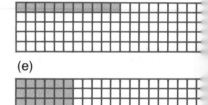

Fig. 20:2

2 100% is another way of saying 'all of them'.

100% of the 500 pupils in Wheatley School are boys. How many boys are there in the school?

3 In his last exam, Bill scored 100%. The total possible mark was 200. How many marks did Bill get?

4 Write as a percentage:

(a) $\frac{24}{100}$    (b) $\frac{30}{100}$    (c) $\frac{80}{100}$    (d) 1 out of 100

(e) 56 out of a 100      (f) 84 out of a hundred

**5 Example** 7% means $\frac{7}{100}$.

Write as a fraction:

(a) 11%    (b) 39%    (c) 9%    (d) 97%

(e) 100%

**6** In Figure 20:3 there are 100 small squares.

6 out of these 100, or $\frac{6}{100}$, or 6%, are shaded.

94 out of these 100, or $\frac{94}{100}$, or 94%, are unshaded.

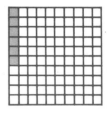
Fig. 20:3

(a) There are 100 small squares in each part of Figure 20:4.
What percentage of each is shaded?

(i)
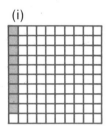

(ii)
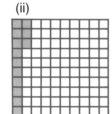

(iii)
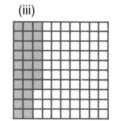

(iv)
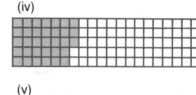

(v)

Fig. 20:4

(b) What percentage of each part of Figure 20:4 is unshaded?

HINT
Do you need to count the little squares?

**7** Alieu says that on his piano 60% of the notes are white and 30% are black. Comment on this.

**8** What percentage is shown on each scale or dial in Figure 20:5?

(a)
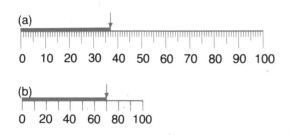

0  10  20  30  40  50  60  70  80  90  100

(b)
0  20  40  60  80  100

Fig. 20:5

(c)
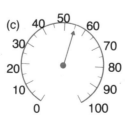

(d)
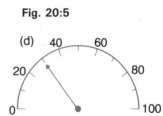

**9** (a) In a school, 40% of the pupils eat a school meal. What percentage do not?

(b) 75% of cats like Catto. What percentage do not?

(c) If 51% of the babies born in 1980 were girls, what percentage were boys?

(d) Mr Brown spends 87% of his wages. What percentage does he save?

(e) If 12% of my garden is lawn, what percentage of my garden is not lawn?

Fig. 20:6

**10** What percentage of a full glass is left in each part of Figure 20:7?

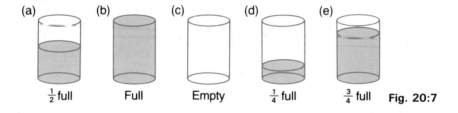

(a) $\frac{1}{2}$ full     (b) Full     (c) Empty     (d) $\frac{1}{4}$ full     (e) $\frac{3}{4}$ full     **Fig. 20:7**

**11** Look at Figure 20:8. What percentage of the original cake is left each day?

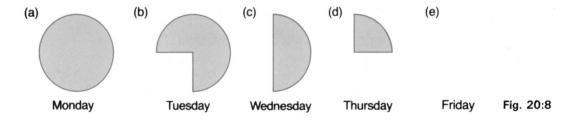

(a) Monday     (b) Tuesday     (c) Wednesday     (d) Thursday     (e) Friday     **Fig. 20:8**

**12 Learn**    100% is the whole of it.
75% is $\frac{3}{4}$ of it.
50% is $\frac{1}{2}$ of it.
25% is $\frac{1}{4}$ of it.
0% is none of it.

**13** What is 50% of:

(a) 12p    (b) 50p    (c) 14 kg    (d) 24 hours

(e) £1?

**14** What is 25% of:

(a) 8p    (b) 20 days    (c) 16 kg    (d) 24 hours

(e) £1?

**15** Using Figure 20:9 to help you, write these percentages as decimals.

(a) 40%    (b) 25%    (c) 48%    (d) 15%

(e) 66%    (f) 92%                         **Fig. 20:9**

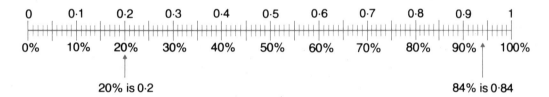

20% is 0·2                            84% is 0·84

**16** Write these decimals as percentages.

(a) 0·3    (b) 0·75    (c) 0·15    (d) 0·48

(e) 0·76    (f) 0·98

**17** Figure 20:10 shows an enlargement of part of Figure 20:9. Use it to help you to write these percentages as decimals.

(a) 3%    (b) 9%    (c) 6%    (d) 2%    (e) 1%

(f) 20%

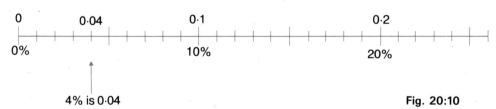

4% is 0·04                                  **Fig. 20:10**

**18** Write these decimals as percentages.

(a) 0·09    (b) 0·07    (c) 0·01    (d) 0·05

(e) 0·15    (f) 0·1

**19** Figure 20:11 shows the numbers of different kinds of crisps sold in a school tuck shop as a percentage of the total number of crisps sold.

| Plain | Salt and vinegar | Curry | Cheese and onion |
|---|---|---|---|

0%  10%  20%  30%  40%  50%  60%  70%  80%  90%  100%

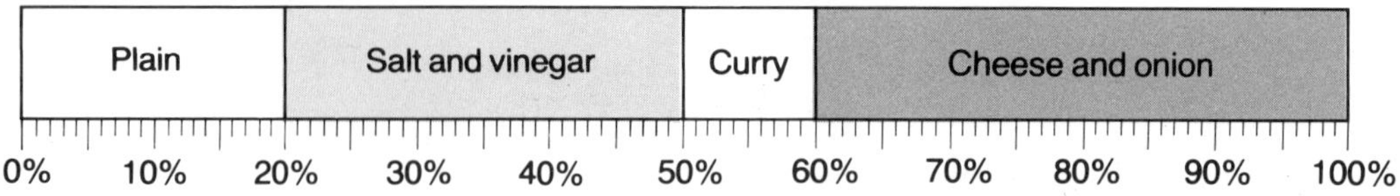

Fig. 20:11

    (a) What percentage of the total number of crisps sold were plain?

    (b) What percentage were salt and vinegar?

    (c) What percentage were curry?

    (d) What percentage were cheese and onion?

**20** Figure 20:12 shows the numbers of different kinds of cars in a car park expressed as a percentage of the total number of cars in the park.

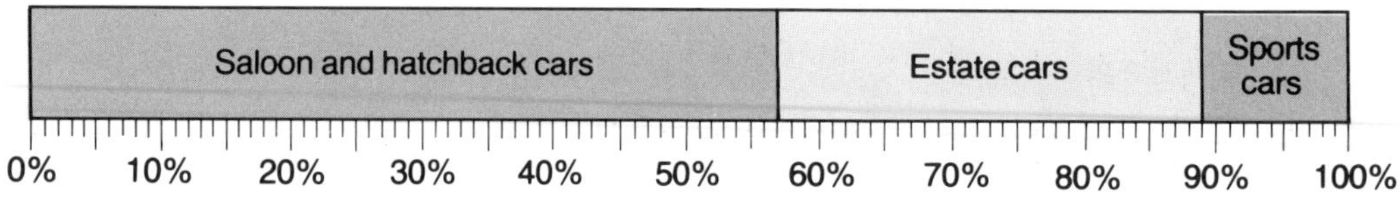

| Saloon and hatchback cars | Estate cars | Sports cars |
|---|---|---|

0%  10%  20%  30%  40%  50%  60%  70%  80%  90%  100%

Fig. 20:12

    What percentage of the total number of cars is each kind of car?

**21** Search through some newspapers. Highlight every percentage that you find.

# B Percentages of money

100 pennies make £1.

So 1 penny is $\frac{1}{100}$ or 1% of £1.

Fig. 20:13

1 **Example.** Find 6p as a percentage of £1.

1p is $\frac{1}{100}$ of £1, or 1% of £1,
so 6p is $\frac{6}{100}$ of £1, or 6% of £1.

Write as a percentage of £1:

(a) 8p    (b) 12p    (c) 22p    (d) 50p    (e) 100p

2 How many pence is:

(a) 1% of £1    (b) 9% of £1    (c) 15% of £1

(d) 24% of £1    (e) 100% of £1?

3 **Example** Find 10% of £3.

10% of £1 is 10p,
so 10% of £3 is 3 times as much,
that is, 3 × 10p = 30p.

(a) Find 10% of £5.    (b) What is 10% of £7?

(c) Work out 10% of £9.    (d) Find 10% of £6.

4 Anita receives 10% of the value of the papers she delivers
to houses. Copy and complete this table to show how much
she earns.

| Day | Value of papers | Wages (10%) |
|---|---|---|
| Monday | £7 | |
| Tuesday | £5 | |
| Wednesday | £9 | |
| Thursday | £10 | |
| Friday | £8 | |
| Saturday | £6 | |
| | Total wages | |

**5 Example**  Find 20% of £3.

        20% of £1 is 20p,
        so 20% of £3 is 3 times as much,
        that is, 3 × 20p = 60p.

(a)  Find 20% of £4.    (b)  What is 20% of £2?

(c)  Work out 20% of £5.    (d)  Find 20% of £7.

**6** Franz receives 20% of the value of the papers he sells on a street corner. Copy and complete the table to show how much he earns.

| Day | Value of papers | Wages (20%) |
|---|---|---|
| Monday | £8 | |
| Tuesday | £10 | |
| Wednesday | £9 | |
| Thursday | £7 | |
| Friday | £11 | |
| Saturday | £14 | |
| Total wages | | |

**7 Note**   30% is the same as 30p in the pound.
            40% is the same as 40p in the pound.

Find:

(a)  30% of £2    (b)  40% of £3    (c)  20% of £4

(d)  30% of £5    (e)  40% of £2    (f)  60% of £3

(g)  80% of £2    (h)  90% of £3

**8  The calculator percentage key**

If your calculator has a percentage key you can use it to do questions like the ones in question 7.

**Example** Find 30% of £2.

2 ⊠ 30 %

Some calculators need = at the end.
Note that you should put in the amount first and
then the percentage of it that you have to find.

If your calculator has no % key you can put in
30% as 0·30 to obtain the same result:

2 ⊠ 0·30 =

Use a calculator to check your answers to question 7.

**9** Use a calculator to find:

(a) 18% of £5     (b) 15% of £9     (c) 8% of £5

(d) 78% of £500     (e) 9% of £54     (f) 7% of £1230

**10** Carmen saves 18% of her £6 pocket money. How much
does she spend?

**11** Regulations state that at least 6% of the people going on
a school trip must be adults. If 60 people are going on a trip,
how many adults must there be?

**12** There are 800 pupils in a school. 47% are boys. How many
girls are there?

**13** A man decides to give 9% of his income to charity. How
much should he give in a week when he earns £230?

**14** Figure 20:14 shows items that a DIY shop will deliver for a
charge of 9% of the price of the item. How much would it
cost to have each item delivered?

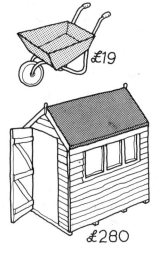
£19

£110

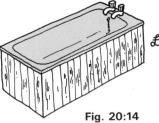

£75

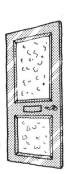
£129

**Fig. 20:14**

£280

**15** Think about the following statements, then write about them.

    (a) Jeremy decides to spend 20% of his week's pocket money on sweets, 25% on comics, 55% in the amusement arcade, and 15% on a present for his sister.

    (b) 55% of a class have been to France and 65% have been to Spain, so 120% of the class have been abroad.

    (c) 68% of the passengers on a plane are going on a holiday. 40% of the passengers are male. 60% of the passengers are females going on holiday.

    (d) Arun and Saul are both given a 8% pay rise. Arun's pay rise is bigger than Saul's.

**16** Make up your own examples of percentage statements for your class to discuss. You might like to use examples from other school subjects.

# C Fraction to percentage

'Per cent' means 'out of a hundred'.
Half of a hundred is $100 \div 2 = 50$, so $\frac{1}{2}$ is 50%.
A quarter of a hundred is $100 \div 4 = 25\%$, so $\frac{1}{4}$ is 25%.

To find $\frac{3}{5}$ as a percentage, first find $\frac{1}{5}$ of a hundred by $100 \div 5 = 20$.
Then $\frac{3}{5}$ is $3 \times 20 = 60$ out of a hundred, or 60%.

To find $\frac{7}{8}$ as a percentage:
$\frac{1}{8}$ of $100 = 100 \div 8 = 12 \cdot 5$
$\frac{7}{8}$ of $100 = 7 \times 12 \cdot 5 = 87 \cdot 5$
So $\frac{7}{8}$ is $87 \cdot 5\%$.

**Note**   The calculator $\boxed{\%}$ key cannot usually be used to change a fraction to a percentage. You can of course use the $\boxed{\div}$ and $\boxed{\times}$ keys to help you work out the answers as in the above examples.

**1** Change to percentages:

    (a) $\frac{3}{4}$     (b) $\frac{2}{5}$     (c) $\frac{17}{100}$     (d) $\frac{9}{10}$     (e) $\frac{3}{10}$

    (f) $\frac{1}{25}$     (g) $\frac{7}{50}$     (h) $\frac{13}{20}$

**2** Use a calculator to help you to change these fractions to percentages to the nearest whole number.

(a) $\frac{1}{3}$    (b) $\frac{2}{3}$    (c) $\frac{8}{9}$    (d) $\frac{7}{11}$    (e) $\frac{7}{23}$

(f) $\frac{2}{17}$    (g) $\frac{81}{93}$    (h) $\frac{77}{111}$

**3** Sharon scores 11 out of 20 ($\frac{11}{20}$) in a test. What is her percentage mark?

**4** 3 out of 20 apples in a box have gone bad. What percentage is this?

**5** 6 out of 40 cars fail the MOT test in a garage in one week.

(a) What percentage is this?

(b) What percentage of the cars tested passed the test?

**6** In a survey, 80 people were asked which make of toothpaste they usually use.
16 said Wonderwhite.
24 said Brill.
36 said whatever was on special offer.
The rest said they did not use any.

Give these results as four percentages.

**7** England forms about $\frac{3}{5}$ of Great Britain.

(a) What percentage is this?

(b) What percentage of Great Britain is **not** England?  .

**8** The air we breathe consists of about $\frac{4}{5}$ nitrogen and $\frac{1}{5}$ oxygen.

(a) What percentage of the air we breathe is nitrogen?

(b) What percentage of the air we breathe is **not** nitrogen? What is it?

**9** One-eighth of an iceberg is above the water level.

(a) What fraction of an iceberg is **below** the water?

(b) What percentage of an iceberg is below the water?

**10** Mark has just completed his first year examinations. He scored:

English: 18 out of 24
Mathematics: 84 out of 120
Science: 48 out of 60
Geography: 21 out of 35
Metalwork: 13 out of 52

It is not easy to see which is the best result when they are all out of different totals.

(a) Change Mark's marks to percentages (so that they are all out of 100).

(b) Write the five subjects in order. Start with the one Mark did best in.

---

**11** Work out the percentage attendance for each member of your class for one week. Design a diagram or a graph to show your information.

**12** Make a class display of examples of percentages used in adverts, magazines, etc. Try to say what each one means.

**13** Write instructions to tell someone how to use the %  key on a calculator.

# A Units of time

▶   ## Points to discuss . . .

1 ▷   **When might you use these?**

| AUGUST | | | |
|---|---|---|---|
| Tue 1 | | | |
| Wed 2 | | | |
| Thur 3 | | | |
| Fri 4 | | | |
| Sat 5 | | | |
| Sun 6 | | | |
| Mon 7 | | | Week 32 |
| Tue 8 | | | |
| Wed 9 | | | |
| Thu 10 | | | |
| Fri 11 | | | |
| Sat 12 | | | |
| Sun 13 | | | |
| Mon 14 | | | Week 33 |
| Tue 15 | | | |
| Wed 16 | | | |
| Thu 17 | | | |
| Fri 18 | | | |
| Sat 19 | | | |
| Sun 20 | | | |
| Mon 21 | | | Week 34 |
| Tue 22 | | | |
| Wed 23 | | | |
| Thu 24 | | | |
| Fri 25 | | | |
| Sat 26 | | | |
| Sun 27 | | | |
| Mon 28 | | | Week 35 |
| Tue 29 | | | |
| Wed 30 | | | |
| Thu 31 | | | |

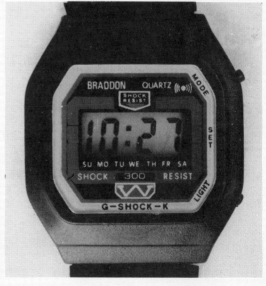

**Fig. 21:1**

2 > What units of time would you use to measure the following times?

(a) boiling an egg    (b) 100 metre sprint

(c) travelling to school    (d) a school term

(e) a maths lesson    (f) your teacher's age

(g) a holiday abroad    (h) the age of the Pyramids

3 > Talk about Figures 21:2 and 21:3.

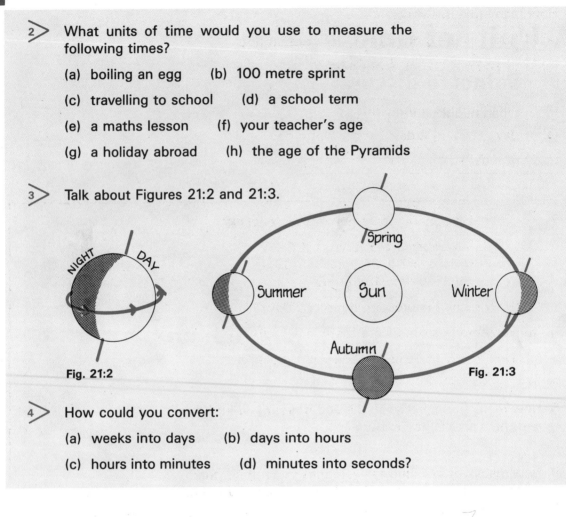

Fig. 21:2    Fig. 21:3

4 > How could you convert:

(a) weeks into days    (b) days into hours

(c) hours into minutes    (d) minutes into seconds?

---

**1** How many days are there in:

(a) 6 weeks    (b) 9 weeks    (c) $\frac{1}{2}$ a week?

**2** How many minutes are there in:

(a) 3 hours    (b) 9 hours    (c) $2\frac{1}{2}$ hours?

**3** How many seconds are there in:

(a) 10 minutes    (b) 5 minutes    (c) $2\frac{1}{2}$ minutes?

**4** How many seconds are there in:

(a) 1 minute    (b) $\frac{1}{2}$ a minute    (c) $\frac{1}{4}$ of a minute

(d) $\frac{3}{4}$ of a minute?

**5** How many minutes make:

    (a) 1 hour    (b) $\frac{1}{2}$ an hour    (c) $\frac{1}{4}$ of an hour

    (d) $\frac{3}{4}$ of an hour    (e) $\frac{1}{3}$ of an hour?

**6** How many hours are there in:

    (a) 1 day    (b) $\frac{1}{2}$ a day    (c) $\frac{3}{4}$ of a day

    (d) $\frac{1}{3}$ of a day?

---

**7 Example** How many hours are there in a week?

        1 week is 1 × 7 days = 7
        7 days is 7 × 24 hours = 168
        So 1 week is 168 hours.

    (a) How many minutes are there in a day?

    (b) How many seconds are there in 1 hour? 60

    (c) How many minutes are there in 1 week? 67

**8** How many hours between the end of your last birthday and the start of the next one?

**9** How many units of time can you find? Write about them. (Here are some to start you off: decade, era, millisecond.)

**10** The light-year is not a unit of time, although it sounds like one. Write about the light-year.

---

# B The 12-hour clock

▶ **Points to discuss . . .**

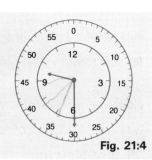

1▷ When looking at a clock face you need to remember that you are looking at two dials, one on top of the other. Figure 21:4 shows this.

2▷ What is meant by a.m. and p.m.? Why are they needed?

**Fig. 21:4**

**1** Write in words and figures the times on the clocks in Figure 21:5.

(a)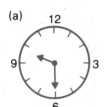

(b)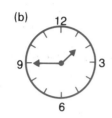

(c)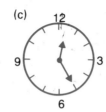

(d)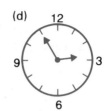

(e)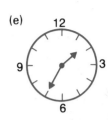

Fig. 21:5

**2** Write in words and figures the times on the clocks in Figure 21:6.

(a)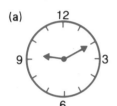

(b)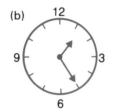

(c)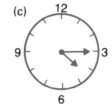

(d)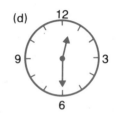

(e)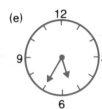

Fig. 21:6

**3** Some early clocks only had an hour hand. You can still tell the time, though not so accurately as with a minute hand too.

Estimate the correct time from the clockfaces in Figure 21:7.

(a)

(b)

(c)

(d)

(e)

Fig. 21:7

**4** A digital clock shows the time in numbers.

Sketch clockfaces and show the position of the hands when the digital time is:

 would look like

Fig. 21:8

(a) 1:15 p.m.    (b) 6:10 a.m.

(c) 5:03 p.m.    (d) 3:09 p.m.

(e) 6:35 p.m.    (f) 7:00 a.m.

(g) 10:49 p.m.    (h) 11:58 p.m.

Worksheet 21A may be used here.

**5** A digital clock changes the display every minute.

Write the next four displays after:

(a) 5:57    (b) 11:58

**6** A countdown clock counts backwards. Write the next four displays on a digital countdown clock starting from:

(a) 7:02 p.m.    (b) 12:03 p.m.

---

Use a clockface to help you do questions 7 and 8.

**7** Eight girls take part in a sponsored silence. Write, in figures, the time when each makes a noise if they start together at 7:40 a.m. and last out for the following times. Ann, 10 min; Babs, 20 min; Cath, 30 min; Di, 45 min; Eva, 50 min; Fay, 2 h 35 min; Gina, 5 h; Helga, 6 h 25 min.

**8** A boy takes 45 minutes to cycle to his friend's house.

When should he set out (in figures) if he wants to arrive at:

(a) 5:50 p.m.    (b) 9:15 p.m.    (c) 6:25 p.m.

(d) half past twelve p.m.    (e) five to six p.m.

(f) ten past one p.m.?

# C Calculations in time

▶ ## Points to discuss . . .

**ROME** by AIRBUS/B.727 of ALITALIA
Weekend arrangements      28/4 to 27/10
Out on Thursday home on Monday
  12.10 dep | HEATHROW ↑ arr 18.05
  15.30 arr ↓    ROME  | dep 16.35
            FIUMICINO
baggage allowance 20 kgs

**VENICE\*** by B.757 of AIR EUROPE
Weekly on Saturday      30/3 to 24/9
  08.15 dep | GATWICK ↑ arr 13.35
  11.15 arr ↓  VENICE  | dep 12.30
baggage allowance 20 kgs

**PISA** by DC9 of ALITALIA
Weekend arrangements      28/4 to 27/10
Out on Thursday home on Monday
  09.00 dep | HEATHROW ↑ arr 18.30
  12.05 arr ↓    PISA   | dep 17.45
baggage allowance 20 kgs

**RIMINI** by B.737 of BRITANNIA AIRWAYS
Weekly on Sunday      22/5 to 11/9
  09.45 dep | GATWICK ↑ arr 14.45
  12.55 arr ↓  RIMINI  | dep 13.40
baggage allowance 20 kgs

Fig. 21:9

Fig. 21:10

**1** Jiang's watch shows that it is 2:47. School ends at 3:20 p.m. How many minutes before Jiang can go home?

**2** Jane starts cooking her frozen dinner at 11:51. The instructions tell her to microwave it for 13 minutes, then let it stand for 5 minutes. At what time will it be ready?

Fig. 21:11

Fig. 21:12

**3** Miguel's train reaches Home Park station at 5:34 p.m. His watch shows 4:10 p.m. How long in hours and minutes before he reaches Home Park?

**4** Sara has organised a treasure hunt. She sends off the six groups of treasure hunters every 8 minutes. The first group leaves at 9:43 a.m. At what times should she send off the other groups?

Fig. 21:13

**5** Anita is cooking rice pilaf in her microwave. The cooking instructions are:

(1) Heat the butter, rice, onion, parsley and celery on HIGH for 3 minutes.

(2) Add remaining ingredients and heat on MEDIUM for 21 minutes.

(3) Stir, cook for 10 more minutes then allow to stand for 5 minutes to finish cooking.

Anita wants the meal ready at 12:15. At what time should she start cooking?

*12.15*
*39*
*11.45*
*15*

**6** The bus for Chorley leaves every hour on the hour. How long will you have to wait for the bus if you arrive at the bus station at:

(a) 9:36    (b) 11:41    (c) 1:16    (d) 9:18

(e) 3:43    (f) 5:11?

Questions 7 to 10 refer to the Radio 2 programme details shown in Figure 21:14.

**7** How long does the afternoon sports programme last?

**8** The Kenny Everett programme lasted 117 minutes. What time did the printer omit to show for 'Oh Mother!'?

**9** How long do the following programmes last, in hours and minutes:

(a) David Jacobs    (b) Big Band Special?    Fig. 21:14

| TWO |
|---|
| **5 00** Peter Marshall: S. |
| **8 02** Racing Bulletin. |
| **8 05** David Jacobs: S. |
| **10 00** Gilbert O'Sullivan, with Star Choice: S. |
| **11 02** Sports Desk. |
| **11 03** Kenny Everett: S. Oh Mother! Rpt. |
| **1 30** Sports, including Doncaster races at **2**, **2.30** and **3.05** (St Leger), plus Classified Results at **5.45**; Athletics; Cricket; Football – Half-time scores at **3.45**, Commentary from **4**, Classified Results at **5** & Pools at **5.50**. |
| **6 00** Country Greats in Concert, rpt. |
| **7 00** Three in a Row. |
| **7 30** Sports Desk. |
| **7 33** Big Band Special: S. |
| **8 00** Robert Farnon's World of Music: S. |
| **9 00** Last Night of the Proms (simultaneous broadcast with BBC 1 TV): S. |
| **10 20** A Century of Music: S, rpt. |
| **11 20** Sports Desk. |
| **11 28** Pete Murray: S. |
| **2 00-5** Richard Clegg: S. |
| VHF: 1 p.m.-7.30 As Radio 1. |

*11.36*
*+ 39*
*1.75*

**10** (a) There are ten stereo (S) programmes. What is their total running time in hours and minutes? (Note: The Kenny Everett programme lasts 117 minutes.)

(b) The Pete Murray programme was on for the same time each Saturday for ten weeks. What was its total running time in hours and minutes?

**11** At Jan's school, Assembly takes 30 minutes. Morning lessons are each 40 minutes, morning break is 20 minutes, afternoon registration is 10 minutes, and afternoon lessons are each 35 minutes. Copy Jan's timetable and write in the starred times.

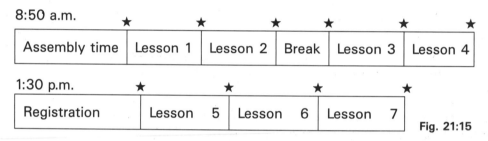

8:50 a.m.

| Assembly time | Lesson 1 | Lesson 2 | Break | Lesson 3 | Lesson 4 |
|---|---|---|---|---|---|

1:30 p.m.

| Registration | Lesson 5 | Lesson 6 | Lesson 7 |
|---|---|---|---|

Fig. 21:15

**12** In question 11:

(a) How long is lunch-break?

(b) How long is spent in lessons each day?

(c) How long is spent in school in a five-day week (including lunch-breaks)?

**13** Make a similar timetable for your school day.

# D The 24-hour clock system

▶ **Points to discuss . . .**

1 ▷ How many times does the hour hand go round on a clockface in one day?

2 ▷ What time should Ian go to the bus station?

Fig. 21:16

**Phone message** ☎

To Ian
From Winston
Meet me at 8'oclock sharp at the bus station

Most timetables now use the 24-hour clock system to avoid problems like those faced by Ian.

The 24-hour clock system numbers the hours of a day from 0, at midnight, right through to 24 hours when it changes back to 0 for the beginning of the next day.

Each day can be shown on a time line, like Figure 21:17.

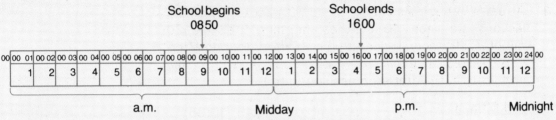

Fig. 21:17

All 24-hour times are written with four figures, so half past three in the morning is 0330 and half past three in the afternoon is 1530.

Here, written as 24-hour times, are the times that Sian starts different activities on one day.

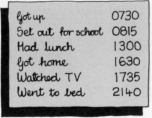

Fig. 21:18

1 **Example**   Twenty to two could be 1:40 a.m. or 1:40 p.m. in the 12-hour clock system, and 0140 or 1340 in the 24-hour clock system.

Write these times as morning and evening times in both the 12-hour clock and the 24-hour clock systems.

(a) eight o'clock      (b) six o'clock      (c) one o'clock

(d) ten o'clock      (e) quarter past two

(f) quarter to nine      (g) five to twelve

2 Write as 24-hour clock times:

(a) 3 a.m.    (b) 7 a.m.    (c) 9 a.m.    (d) 11 a.m.

(e) 3 p.m.    (f) 7 p.m.    (g) 9:15 a.m.

(h) 7:45 p.m.    (i) twenty to eight p.m.

**3** Write as a.m./p.m. times:

(a) 0800    (b) 0600    (c) 1400    (d) 2300

(e) 0516    (f) 1824

**4** Copy and complete these tables.

### Morning (a.m.)

| 12-hour time | 4:20 | 5:35 | 6:42 | | | | 11:15 |
|---|---|---|---|---|---|---|---|
| 24-hour time | | | | 0700 | 0920 | 1036 | |

### Afternoon/evening (p.m.)

| 12-hour time | 1:20 | | 3:04 | | 9:15 | 10:35 | |
|---|---|---|---|---|---|---|---|
| 24-hour time | 1320 | 1404 | | 1806 | | | 2321 |

---

**5**    **Paignton and Dartmouth Steam Railway**

| Paignton dep. | 1030 | 1200 | 1430 | 1600 |
|---|---|---|---|---|
| Goodrington | 1035 | 1205 | 1435 | 1605 |
| Churston | 1045 | 1215 | 1445 | 1615 |
| Kingswear arr. | 1100 | 1230 | 1500 | 1630 |
| Kingswear dep. | 1115 | 1245 | 1515 | 1700 |
| Churston | 1130 | 1300 | 1530 | 1715 |
| Goodrington | 1040 | 1310 | 1540 | 1725 |
| Paignton arr. | 1045 | 1315 | 1545 | 1730 |

Starting at Paignton, plan a day out on the railway. On your plan write down which trains you will catch and when you will arrive at your destinations.

# E The calendar

Thirty days hath September, April, June and November.
All the rest have thirty-one excepting February alone
Which has but twenty-eight days clear
        or twenty-nine in a leap year.

1 How many days are there in:

(a) May     (b) December     (c) April     (d) October

(e) June?

2 (a) How many days are there in a week?

(b) How many weeks are there in a year?

(c) Is your answer to part (b) exact? If not, how many days are left over in a normal year?

3 Which of the following were leap years?
1944,   1973,   1978,   1980,   1958,   1952

4 **Example**   21st June 1972 can be written 21.6.72.
            (June is the 6th month.)
Write in full:

(a) 18.10.43     (b) 25.6.69     (c) 25.7.66

5 Write in figures:

(a) 21st Jan. 1964     (b) 10th May 1968

(c) 21st Nov. 1969

6 If 1st Feb. is a Friday, what day is:

(a) 5th Feb.     (b) 8th Feb.     (c) 15th Feb.     (d) 27th Feb.?

7 Write the months of the year in order, saying how many days there are in each.

8 Write in figures:

(a) 4th May 1976     (b) 21st March 1970

(c) 31st December 1974     (d) 16 June 1978

(e) 14 February 1974     (f) July 2nd 1941

**9** Write in full:

(a) 6.4.75    (b) 9.8.71    (c) 8.11.51    (d) 18.11.81

(e) 11.11.11

**10** Which of the following were leap years?
1904,  1937,  1948,  1950,  1960,  1982

**11** If May 3rd is a Sunday, what day that year is:

(a) May 10th    (b) May 19th    (c) June 1st?

Worksheet 21B may be used here.

---

**12** January 1st 1981 was a Thursday. What day was January 1st in 1982?

**13** Write the next leap year after each of the years in question 10.

**14** Christmas Day 1979 was a Tuesday. On what day was Christmas Day in:

(a) 1980    (b) 1981?

**15** The pirate Captain Kidd was born on 10th June 1645. He was hanged on 23rd May 1701. How many years old was he when he died?

**16** How many days are there *inclusively* (that is, including the ones given) from:

(a) 3rd June to 6th June (*not* 3 days)

(b) 1st March to 21st May

(c) 1st July to 10th September

(d) 8th August to 9th December

(e) 10th December to 11th January

(f) 9.7.91 to 2.2.92?

**17** Find out which calendar uses only 354 days and write about it.

# A Rounding numbers

▶ **Points to discuss . . .**

Which amounts in Figure 22:1 are **exact** and which are **approximate**? How approximate do you think they are, e.g. the nearest 1; the nearest 100?

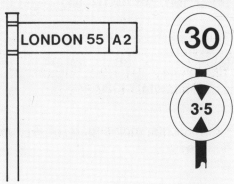

Fig. 22:1

The following examples show you how to round numbers.

**If the 'key figure' is 5 or more, increase the figure in front of it by 1.**

Example   Round 624 to the nearest ten.
$$\begin{array}{ccc} H & T & U \\ 6 & 2 & 4 \end{array} \to 620$$
tens figure   key figure

Round 746 to the nearest ten.
$$\begin{array}{ccc} H & T & U \\ 7 & 4 & 6 \end{array} \to 750$$
tens figure   key figure

Round 8248 to the nearest hundred.
$$\begin{array}{cccc} Th & H & T & U \\ 8 & 2 & 4 & 8 \end{array} \to 8200$$
hundreds figure   key figure

**1** Figure 22:2 shows part of a number line divided into tens.

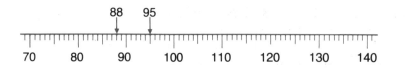

Fig. 22:2

88 is nearer to 90 than to 80. We round 88 to 90 correct to the nearest ten.

95 is halfway between 90 and 100. It could be rounded to 90 or 100, but we usually round up, to 100.

Round to the nearest ten:

(a) 72     (b) 86     (c) 94     (d) 125     (e) 137

(f)  115     (g) 103

**2** Figure 22:3 shows part of a number line divided into hundreds.

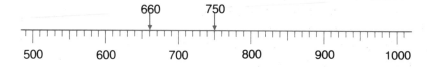

Fig. 22:3

660 is nearer to 700 than to 600. We round 660 to 700 correct to the nearest hundred.

750 is halfway between 700 and 800. It could be rounded to 700 or 800, but we usually round up, to 800.

Round to the nearest hundred:

(a) 580     (b) 620     (c) 850     (d) 910     (e) 75

(f)  960     (g) 880

**3 Examples**    2300 is 2000 correct to the nearest 1000.

2519 is 3000 correct to the nearest 1000.

Round to the nearest thousand:

(a) 1800     (b) 2200     (c) 4800     (d) 1500

(e) 700     (f)  500     (g) 200

**4** Copy and complete this table.

| Number | 26 | 42 | 78 | 126 | 141 | 258 | 924 | 2436 |
|---|---|---|---|---|---|---|---|---|
| to nearest 10 | | | | | | | | |

**5** Copy and complete this table.

| Number | 726 | 4841 | 7264 | 946 | 881 | 1160 | 5243 | 150 |
|---|---|---|---|---|---|---|---|---|
| to nearest 100 | | | | | | | | |

**6** Copy and complete this table.

| Number | 8264 | 9401 | 18 206 | 99 449 | 3526 | 4710 |
|---|---|---|---|---|---|---|
| to nearest 1000 | | | | | | |

**7** Look at newspapers, magazines, catalogues, labels and leaflets for numbers in print. Cut them out or copy them and make a display saying whether you think the numbers or amounts are exact or approximate.

# B Using approximations

▶ ## Points to discuss . . .

1 > Figure 22:4 shows people using approximations. What approximations do you use?

Fig. 22:4

2 > What sort of approximations do people in different jobs use?

**1** Figure 22:5 shows a scale representing £1. You can see that 27p to the nearest ten pence is 30p.

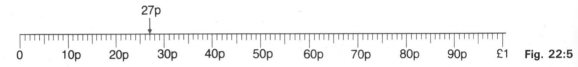

27p

Fig. 22:5

Write to the nearest ten pence:

(a) 48p    (b) 36p    (c) 24p    (d) 93p

(e) 55p    (f) 37p    (g) 75p

**2** Write to the nearest ten pence:

(a) £0·38    (b) £0·72    (c) £0·56    (d) £0·15

(e) £0·88    (f) £0·95    (g) £0·66

**3** When shopping in a supermarket it is useful to know roughly how much you have spent. You can do this by approximating each price to the nearest ten pence, which makes it easier to add up.

**Example**  48p, call it 50p
16p, call it 20p
4p, ignore it
76p, call it 80p
33p, call it 30p
£2·12, call it £2·10

The approximate cost is 50p + 20p + 80p + 30p + £2·10, giving £3·90.

What is the exact cost of the goods in the example?

Fig. 22:6

**4** By rounding each price to the nearest ten pence find **roughly** the total bill for the following. (Do the work in your head if you can.)

(a) 37p + 51p + 69p + 12p

(b) 47p + 82p + 76p + 33p

(c) £1·39 + £1·52

(d) £1·77 + £1·44 + £1·18 + £1·53

(e) 38p + £1·26 + £1·71 + 47p + £1·62 + 72p

**5** Calculate the exact totals for question 4, and the differences between your approximations and the true amounts.

**6** **Example** 44p × 18 is roughly 40p × 20 = 800p or £8·00.
We can write this as 44p × 18 ≈ £8·00.

Find an approximate value for:

(a) 59p × 11    (b) 33p × 29    (c) 38p × 13

(d) 69p × 22    (e) 52p × 37

**7** Find the exact answers for question 6, and the differences between your approximations and the true amounts.

**8** These are answers to money problems on a calculator. Write each answer correct to the nearest £1.

(a) 3.89   (b) 1.42   (c) 0.77

(d) 9.95   (e) 1.57   (f) 4.34

(g) 0.65   (h) 7.96          Fig. 22:7

**9** These are answers to money problems on a calculator. Write each answer as an amount you could pay in a shop.

(a) 5.118   (b) 3.6   (c) 4.225

(d) 6.2857142   (e) 1.5   (f) 7.375

(g) 6.6666666   (h) 0.875          Fig. 22:8

10 Rewrite the following statements, rounding the numbers as told.

   (a) There are 867 pupils in our school. (Round to the nearest 10.)

   (b) My anorak cost £9·99. (Round to the nearest £1.)

   (c) The attendance at the football match was 27 601. (Round to the nearest 1000.)

   (d) There are 2855 books in the school library. (Round to the nearest 100.)

   (e) My weekly newsagents bill is £4·76. (Round to the nearest 10p.)

   (f) I have 1385 stamps in my collection. (Round to the nearest 10.)

   (g) We travelled 758 miles on our holiday. (Round to the nearest 100.)

   (h) There are 14 761 people in Ballyville. (Round to the nearest 1000.

11 Copy and complete this table. Be careful to round to the nearest *thousand.*

| Ground | Spurs | Forest | Stoke | Luton | Villa | Total crowd |
|---|---|---|---|---|---|---|
| Crowd exactly | 28 746 | 48 231 | 32 421 | 41 646 | 24 349 | exactly |
| Crowd to the nearest 1000 | | | | | | roughly |

12 A litre of paint covers about 9 m². How many litres should be bought to give two coats of paint to a wall:

   (a) 15 m by 3 m    (b) 13 m by 4 m?

13 'I am 184 cm 8·26 mm tall' is a silly thing to say. Why? What would be more sensible?

**14** An approximation for the area of an irregular shape can be found by counting squares inside it. A square is counted only if more than half of it is inside the shape. Find approximations for the areas of the leaves in Figure 22:9, first by counting using the centimetre squares, then more accurately by using the small squares. Each small square is $\frac{1}{25}$ cm$^2$ or 0·04 cm$^2$. Put a piece of tracing paper over the diagrams to avoid marking the book.

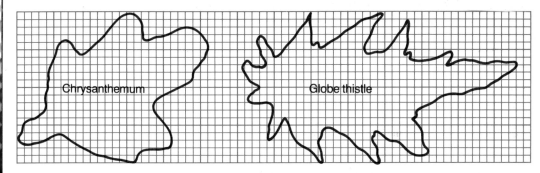

Chrysanthemum

Globe thistle

Fig. 22:9

**15** Write some sentences to describe what would happen if all the prices in your nearest supermarket were rounded to the nearest ten pence.

# Decimal fractions: division by 10; 100; 1000

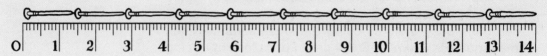

This line of 10 nails is 14 cm long.

Each nail is 14 cm ÷ 10 = 1·4 cm long.

Fig. 23:1

| 100 | 10 | 1 | $\frac{1}{10}$ | $\frac{1}{100}$ | $\frac{1}{1000}$ |
|---|---|---|---|---|---|
|  | 1 | 4 • |  |  |  |

divide by 10 ⟶

| 100 | 10 | 1 | $\frac{1}{10}$ | $\frac{1}{100}$ | $\frac{1}{1000}$ |
|---|---|---|---|---|---|
|  |  | 1 • | 4 |  |  |

To divide by 10, move the figures one column to the right. (Moving figures one column to the right makes them worth a tenth as much.)

**Further examples**

| 100 | 10 | 1 | $\frac{1}{10}$ | $\frac{1}{100}$ | $\frac{1}{1000}$ |
|---|---|---|---|---|---|
|  | 3 | 7 • | 5 |  |  |
| 4 | 2 | 6 • |  |  |  |
| 3 | 5 | 0 • |  |  |  |
|  |  | 1 • | 4 |  |  |

divide by 10 ⟶

| 100 | 10 | 1 | $\frac{1}{10}$ | $\frac{1}{100}$ | $\frac{1}{1000}$ |
|---|---|---|---|---|---|
|  |  | 3 • | 7 | 5 |  |
|  | 4 | 2 • | 6 |  |  |
|  | 3 | 5 • | 0 |  |  |
|  |  | 0 • | 1 | 4 |  |

**1** Show these divisions in the same way as the examples above.

(a)  42·5 ÷ 10     (b)  1·8 ÷ 10     (c)  375 ÷ 10

(d)  15 ÷ 10

**2** Write answers to the following:

(a)  25·8 ÷ 10     (b)  37 ÷ 10     (c)  178 ÷ 10

(d)  390 ÷ 10     (e)  96 ÷ 10     (f)  15·6 ÷ 10

(g)  4·8 ÷ 10     (h)  27·3 ÷ 10     (i)  6 ÷ 10

(j)  2·5 ÷ 10

**3 Example**    $0 \cdot 4 \div 10 = 0 \cdot 04$
You need to write an extra zero in front of the decimal point.

Write answers to the following:

(a)  $0 \cdot 2 \div 10$     (b)  $4 \div 10$     (c)  $0 \cdot 9 \div 10$

(d)  $0 \cdot 65 \div 10$     (e)  $0 \cdot 1 \div 10$     (f)  $7 \div 10$

(g)  $0 \cdot 6 \div 10$     (h)  $0 \cdot 88 \div 10$     (i)  $1 \div 10$

(j)  $0 \cdot 05 \div 10$

**4** A strip of 10 postage stamps is 16 cm wide. How wide is each stamp?

Fig. 23:2

←————————————————— 16 cm —————————————————→

**5** A pile of 10 coins is $5 \cdot 2$ cm high. How thick is one coin?

5·2 cm

Fig. 23:3

**6** A path is made of 10 paving slabs. The path is $9 \cdot 5$ m long. What is the width of one slab?

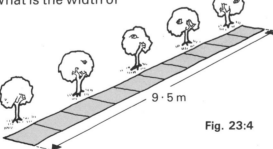

9·5 m

Fig. 23:4

**7** A pile of 10 playing cards is $0 \cdot 8$ cm high. How thick is one card?

**8** 10 kg of sausages cost £19·40. What is the cost of 1 kg of sausages?

**9** This line of 100 pin heads is 14 cm long. Each pin head is
14 cm ÷ 100 = 0·14 cm.

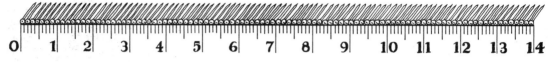

Fig. 23:5

| 100 | 10 | 1 | $\frac{1}{10}$ | $\frac{1}{100}$ | $\frac{1}{1000}$ |
|---|---|---|---|---|---|
|  | 1 | 4 • |  |  |  |

divide by
100
⟶

| 100 | 10 | 1 | $\frac{1}{10}$ | $\frac{1}{100}$ | $\frac{1}{1000}$ |
|---|---|---|---|---|---|
|  |  | 0 • | 1 | 4 |  |

To divide by 100, move the figures two columns to the right.
(Moving figures two columns to the right makes them worth
a hundredth as much.)

**Further examples**

| 100 | 10 | 1 | $\frac{1}{10}$ | $\frac{1}{100}$ | $\frac{1}{1000}$ |
|---|---|---|---|---|---|
| 1 | 5 | 6 • |  |  |  |
| 3 | 2 | 7 • | 4 |  |  |
|  | 6 | 0 • |  |  |  |
|  |  | 5 • |  |  |  |

divide by
100
⟶
⟶
⟶
⟶

| 100 | 10 | 1 | $\frac{1}{10}$ | $\frac{1}{100}$ | $\frac{1}{1000}$ |
|---|---|---|---|---|---|
|  |  | 1 • | 5 | 6 |  |
|  |  | 3 • | 2 | 7 | 4 |
|  |  | 0 • | 6 |  |  |
|  |  | 0 • | 0 | 5 |  |

Show these divisions in the same way as the examples
above.

(a) 25 ÷ 100  (b) 268 ÷ 100  (c) 505 ÷ 100

(d) 7 ÷ 100

**10** Write answers to the following:

(a) 314 ÷ 100  (b) 260 ÷ 100  (c) 85 ÷ 100

(d) 19 ÷ 100  (e) 47·5 ÷ 100  (f) 600 ÷ 100

(g) 6 ÷ 100  (b) 1 ÷ 100  (i) 458 ÷ 100

(j) 45 ÷ 100

**11** 100 pennies weigh 350 g. What is the weight of one penny?

Fig. 23:6

**12** A pile of 100 sheets of card is 175 mm high. How thick is one sheet of card?

**13** 100 ballpoint pens cost £45. What is the cost of one pen?

**14** 100 tins of paint cost £349. What is the cost of one tin?

**15** 100 wire coat hangers can be made from 85 m of wire. How much wire is needed for one coat hanger?

Fig. 23:7

**16** 1000 butterbeans weigh 900 grams. Each bean weighs 900 grams ÷ 1000 = 0·9 g.

*Do all the butter beans really weigh the same?*

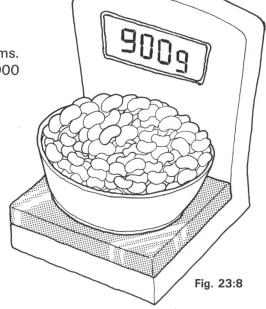

Fig. 23:8

| 100 | 10 | 1 | $\frac{1}{10}$ | $\frac{1}{100}$ | $\frac{1}{1000}$ | divide by 1000 | 100 | 10 | 1 | $\frac{1}{10}$ | $\frac{1}{100}$ | $\frac{1}{1000}$ |
|-----|----|----|----|----|----|----|----|----|----|----|----|----|
| 9 | 0 | 0● | | | | ⟶ | | ●0 | | 9 | 0 | 0 |

To divide by 1000, move the figures three columns to the right. (Moving figures three columns to the right makes them worth a thousandth as much.)

**Further examples**

| 100 | 10 | 1 | $\frac{1}{10}$ | $\frac{1}{100}$ | $\frac{1}{1000}$ |
|---|---|---|---|---|---|
| 8 | 7 | 5 • | | | |
| 2 | 5 | 0 • | | | |
| | 6 | 4 • | | | |
| | | 8 • | | | |

divide by 1000 ⟶

| 100 | 10 | 1 | $\frac{1}{10}$ | $\frac{1}{100}$ | $\frac{1}{1000}$ |
|---|---|---|---|---|---|
| | | 0 • | 8 | 7 | 5 |
| | | 0 • | 2 | 5 | |
| | | 0 • | 0 | 6 | 4 |
| | | 0 • | 0 | 0 | 8 |

Show these divisions in the same way as the examples above.

(a) 625 ÷ 1000     (b) 72 ÷ 1000     (c) 7 ÷ 1000

(d) 60 ÷ 1000

**17** Write answers to the following:

(a) 475 ÷ 1000     (b) 666 ÷ 1000     (c) 105 ÷ 1000

(d) 6 ÷ 1000     (e) 67 ÷ 1000     (f) 1 ÷ 1000

(g) 80 ÷ 1000     (h) 360 ÷ 1000     (i) 40 ÷ 1000

(j) 9 ÷ 1000

**18** 1000 paper clips weigh 350 grams. What is the weight of each paper clip?

**19** 1000 tap washers cost £120. What is the cost of one tap washer?

Fig. 23:9

**20** 1000 aspirin tablets weigh 200 g. What is the weight of one tablet?

**21 Remember** Moving figures one column to the right makes them worth a tenth as much.

Moving figures two columns to the right makes them worth a hundredth as much.

Moving figures three columns to the right makes them worth a thousandth as much.

Find:

(a)  48 ÷ 10     (b)  154 ÷ 10     (c)  65 ÷ 100

(d)  875 ÷ 1000     (e)  8 ÷ 10     (f)  645 ÷ 100

(g)  700 ÷ 1000     (h)  7 ÷ 100     (i)  1 ÷ 1000

(j)  105 ÷ 10     (k)  82 ÷ 100     (l)  50 ÷ 1000

---

**22** Measure the height of 100 pieces of paper, and so calculate the thickness of one piece of paper.

**23** Find the thickness of each of our coins.

**24** Find the thickness of a cotton thread.

100 turns

Length

Fig. 23:10

# Statistics: the mean

When Patrick was asked how much pocket money he received he was not sure how to answer. One way would have been to work out an average called the **mean**.

The mean is found by dividing the sum of the items by the number of items, so for Patrick his mean pocket money was $(£2 + £5 + £1 + £4) ÷ 4 = £12 ÷ 4 = £3$.

If he had received £3 each week for the four weeks he would have received the same total amount of £12.

This month I was given £2, £5, £1 and £4.

Fig. 24:1

There are three statistical averages:

- the **mean** is the amount found by sharing out the total equally.
- the **mode** is the most popular amount.
- the **median** has half the amounts above it and half below it.

In newspapers it is often not clear which of these averages is being used.

In mathematics we assume that the mean is meant when the word average is used, unless we are told otherwise.

**Example**   Find the mean of 2, 4, 4, 8, 8, 10.

The total is $2 + 4 + 4 + 8 + 8 + 10 = 36$

The mean is $36 ÷ 6 = 6$

**1**  Find the mean of:

(a)  2, 5, 3, 6      (b)  2, 10, 7, 5, 6      (c)  7, 1, 2, 2, 1, 5

(d)  12, 15, 16, 13      (e)  7, 24, 11, 13, 15

(f)  24, 13, 19, 14, 19, 67      (g)  27, 49, 31, 33, 30

**2**  Find the mean weekly pocket money for Franz, Derek, Gustave, Fatima and Ruby.

| Franz | £2 | £5 | £1 | £4 |
|---|---|---|---|---|
| Derek | £2 | £2 | £2 | £2 |
| Gustave | £4 | £3 | £4 | £1 |
| Fatima | £5 | £4 | £4 | £3 |
| Ruby | £1 | £2 | £4 | £5 |

**3** (a) Work out each team's mean number of goals scored per match, called the 'goal average'. Give your answer as a decimal fraction, like 3·4.

(b) Position the teams 1st to 4th based on goal average.

| Team | Goals scored in ten matches |
|------|------------------------------|
| Atoms | 1, 4, 1, 2, 3, 5, 2, 1, 0, 1 |
| Breakers | 2, 2, 3, 1, 4, 0, 0, 2, 1, 2 |
| Cheats | 3, 0, 1, 2, 0, 4, 2, 9, 3, 1 |
| Dragons | 0, 4, 1, 4, 2, 1, 3, 1, 4, 2 |

**4** (a) Find the total weight of these five boxes.

(b) Find the mean weight of the boxes.

(c) Which boxes weigh more than the mean?

(d) Which boxes weigh less than the mean?

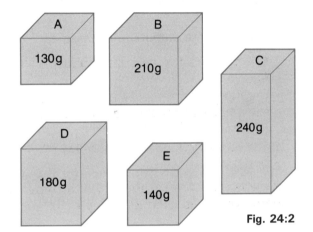

Fig. 24:2

**5** (a) Find the total cost of these shoe cleaners.

(b) Find the mean cost of the cleaners.

(c) How many of the cleaners cost more than the mean?

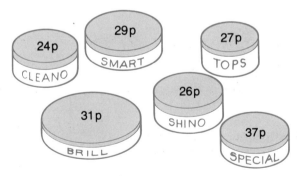

Fig. 24:3

**6** Find the mean of:

(a) 2, 5, 9, 4, 10     (b) 7, 12, 8, 6, 9, 12

(c) 13, 17, 15, 14, 16     (d) 7, 2, 6, 5, 9, 8, 12, 3, 4, 2

(e) 1, 9, 8, 2, 7, 5, 9, 6, 9, 12

**7** The table shows the marks scored by seven pupils on ten tests.

**Example** Liz scored a total of 62 marks, so her average was 62 ÷ 10 = 6·2.

(a) Work out the mean marks for the other pupils.

(b) Position the pupils in order from 1st to 7th, based on their average score.

| | Test | | | | | | | | | |
|---|---|---|---|---|---|---|---|---|---|---|
| | 1 | 2 | 3 | 4 | 5 | 6 | 7 | 8 | 9 | 10 |
| Liz | 6 | 5 | 7 | 8 | 6 | 6 | 5 | 4 | 7 | 8 |
| Ann | 5 | 8 | 7 | 7 | 8 | 5 | 7 | 6 | 4 | 7 |
| Jill | 8 | 10 | 10 | 8 | 7 | 6 | 5 | 8 | 4 | 9 |
| Dick | 7 | 8 | 10 | 10 | 8 | 9 | 9 | 8 | 2 | 6 |
| Tony | 6 | 7 | 5 | 7 | 4 | 3 | 7 | 6 | 5 | 4 |
| Alan | 4 | 8 | 7 | 7 | 6 | 5 | 8 | 9 | 8 | 10 |
| Jim | 7 | 3 | 6 | 7 | 6 | 4 | 5 | 5 | 8 | 4 |

**8** Figure 24:4 shows the attendance of a class for one school week.

(a) Find the attendance each day.

(b) Find the mean attendance for the week.

(c) Which days were above the mean?

**9** Find the mean of:

(a) 6, 7, 8, 9, 10

(b) 11, 12, 13, 14, 15

(c) 8, 9, 10, 11, 12, 13, 14

**10** What do you notice about your three answers to question 9?

**11** Figure 24:5 shows the noon temperature at Sunsea from the 7th to the 16th of August last year. Read each day's temperature, then calculate the mean temperature to the nearest whole number.

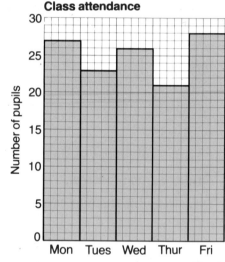

Class attendance

Fig. 24:4

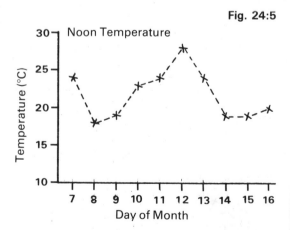

Fig. 24:5

Noon Temperature

**12** The contents of twelve boxes of matches were counted. The results were: 51, 46, 50, 42, 43, 52, 47, 49, 46, 53, 54, 43.

(a) Find the average (mean) contents of the boxes.

(b) Why do the manufacturers put 'average contents 48' on the boxes? Are they being honest?

Fig. 24:6

**13** The costs of different makes of office computers are £1014·58, £964·13, £1428·72 and £1073·77. Find the average cost.

**14**

|  | Bags of cement sold | | | | | |
|---|---|---|---|---|---|---|
|  | Mon | Tues | Wed | Thur | Fri | Sat |
| Week 1 | 126 | 127 | 30 | 163 | 421 | 210 |
| Week 2 | 128 | 135 | 67 | 175 | 270 | 115 |
| Week 3 | 112 | 140 | 75 | 186 | 264 | 136 |
| Week 4 | 114 | 148 | 80 | 195 | 288 | 244 |

The table shows the number of bags of cement sold at a builders' merchant over four weeks.

(a) Calculate the mean number of bags sold each week. Give your answers to the nearest whole number.

(b) Calculate the mean number of bags sold each day. Give your answers to the nearest hundred.

**15** Find the mean number of pets owned by pupils in your class.

## A Rectangular numbers

8 can be represented by eight dots. • • • • • • • •

These eight dots can be set out in a rectangle. • • • •
• • • •

We say that 8 is therefore a **rectangular number**.

7 is not a rectangular number because it cannot be set out as a rectangle of dots.

**1** Make rectangle patterns for:

(a) 6　　(b) 8　　(c) 10　　(d) 14　　(e) 15

**2** Make, if possible, rectangle patterns for:

(a) 21　　(b) 11　　(c) 17　　(d) 27　　(e) 13

**3** Some numbers can be set out as a rectangle of dots in more than one way. The numbers in brackets tell you how many different ones can be made. Draw them all for:

(a) 12 (2)　　(b) 18 (2)　　(c) 20 (2)　　(d) 24 (3)

(e) 42 (3)

**4** Which rectangular numbers smaller than 50 can be drawn as four different rectangles?

Investigate further.

## B Square numbers

16 can be represented by sixteen dots.

• • • • • • • • • • • • • • • •

These sixteen dots can be set out in a rectangle.

• • • • • • • •
• • • • • • • •

They can also be set out as a square.

• • • •
• • • •
• • • •
• • • •

We say that 16 is therefore a **square number**.

**1** Make, if possible, rectangle and square patterns for:

    (a) 4      (b) 6     (c) 7     (d) 9     (e) 12     (f) 16

    (g) 20    (h) 22    (i) 25    (j) 36

**2** Find the first twenty square numbers.
Write your answers like this:    $1 \times 1 = 1$
                                            $2 \times 2 = 4$
                                            $3 \times 3 = 9$

**3** Look at your list of square numbers in question 2.

    (a) Take the first square number from the second.

    (b) Take the second square number from the third.

    (c) Take the third square number from the fourth, and so on. What do you notice about your answers?

**4** What do you notice about the digits in the units column for your list of square numbers?

**5** Here is a square of dots growing:

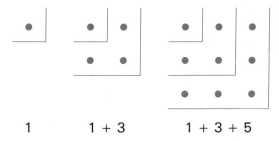

    1            1 + 3        1 + 3 + 5

Copy these patterns, and continue them, at least to 25 dots, further if you like.

**6** Look back to your work in question 5. Write about square numbers and odd numbers.

---

**7** (a) Find three square numbers that add up to 21.

    (b) Find three square numbers that add up to 33.

    (c) Find four square numbers that add up to 79.

    (d) Investigate other numbers made by adding square numbers. Can you find any numbers that cannot be made by adding squares? Can you find any numbers that need more than four squares?

# C Triangular numbers

Triangular numbers can be represented by a triangle of dots:

1 ●          The first triangular number is 1.
3 ● ●       The second triangular number is 3.
6 ● ● ●    The third triangular number is 6.

**1** Write the first ten triangular numbers in a column, using equally spaced dots to illustrate them.

**2** (a) Add the first and second triangular numbers.

(b) Add the second and third triangular numbers.

(c) Add the third and fourth triangular numbers.

(d) Add the fourth and fifth triangular numbers, and so on. What do you notice about your answers?

**3** All square numbers can be made by adding two consecutive triangular numbers. For example, 16 can be made from 6 and 10 as shown in Figure 25:1.

$$10 \quad + \quad 6 \quad = \quad 16$$

Fig. 25:1

Draw five squares of dots and crosses to show how the square numbers from 9 to 49 can be made by adding two triangular numbers.

**4** Copy this and continue it for squares up to 100.

| Squares | Triangular |
|---------|------------|
| 1 | = 1 |
| 4 | = 1 + 3 |
| 9 | = 3 + 6 |
| 16 | = 6 + 10 |

**5** (a) Find two triangular numbers that add up to 38.

(b) Find three triangular numbers that add up to 32.

(c) Find three triangular numbers that add up to 44.

(d) Find three triangular numbers that add up to 30. (You can use the same number several times.)

(e) Investigate other numbers made by adding triangular numbers. Can you find any numbers that cannot be made by adding triangular numbers? Can you find any numbers that need more than three triangular numbers?

# D Factors

How many people can six tennis balls be shared among?

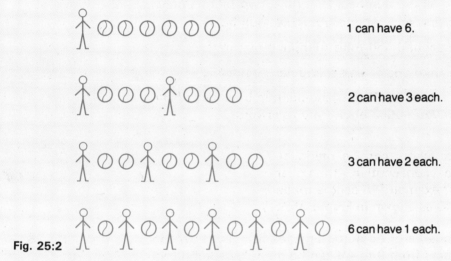

1 can have 6.

2 can have 3 each.

3 can have 2 each.

6 can have 1 each.

Fig. 25:2

Integers which multiply by another integer to make a given number are called **factors** of that number.

Example    6 is a factor of 30 because 6 × 5 = 30.

6 is not a factor of 15 because $6 \times 2\frac{1}{2} = 15$, and $2\frac{1}{2}$ is not an integer.

We can also say that 6 is a factor of 30 because 30 ÷ 6 is an integer, and that 6 is not a factor of 15 because 15 ÷ 6 is not an integer.

1  Example    List the factors of 50.
              Answer:    1, 2, 5, 10, 25, 50.

List the factors of the following. The numbers in brackets tell you how many factors to find.

(a)  5  (2)        (b)  8  (4)        (c)  10  (4)        (d)  12  (6)

(e)  18  (6)

**2 Example**  Write 12 as the product of two factors in as many ways as you can.

Answer:  1 × 12
2 × 6
3 × 4

Write these as the product of two factors in as many ways as you can:

(a) 8    (b) 18    (c) 20    (d) 24    (e) 30

**3** Copy and complete the table for factors of numbers from 1 to 50. Ring all the numbers that have two factors only.

| Number | Factors |
|--------|---------|
| 1 | 1 |
| ② | 1, 2 |
| ③ | 1, 3 |
| 4 | 1, 2, 4 |
| ⑤ | 1, 5 |
| 6 | 1, 2, 3, 6 |
| ⑦ | 1, 7 |
| 8 | 1, 2, 4, 8 |

and so on.

**4** How many people can 60 tennis balls be shared among?
Make some drawings like Figure 25:2.

Figure 26:1 is a drawing of a room looking from above it. It is called a **scale plan** of the room, and is exactly the same shape as the room but smaller.

Fig. 26:1

The scale used is 1 cm represents 1 m.
The drawing is 4 cm long, so the room is 4 m long.
The drawing is 3 cm wide, so the room is 3 m wide.

We can write scales in several ways. For Figure 26:1 we could say:

- 1 cm represents 1 m
- 1 cm represents 100 cm
- The scale is 1 : 100

*Read this as '1 to a hundred'.*

1 (a)  Measure the diagonal of Figure 26:1 (across the rectangle from corner to corner).

  (b)  What is the length of the same diagonal in the actual room?

2  On 1 cm squared paper, using the scale 1 : 100 draw scale drawings like Figure 26:1 to represent:

  (a)  a square flower-bed whose side is 5 m long

  (b)  a rectangular garden pool, 10 m long and 6 m wide

  (c)  a rectangular garage, 9 m long and 3 m wide

3  Draw a diagonal on each of your scale drawings and so calculate the lengths of the diagonals of the flower-bed, the pool, and the garage.

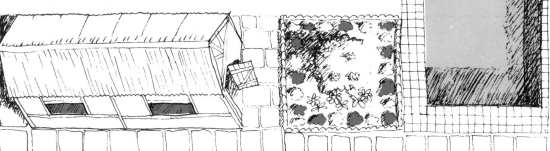

4  Figure 26:2 is a scale plan of a flat. The scale is 1 : 100. Copy
   and complete the table to show the true measurements of
   the rooms in the flat.

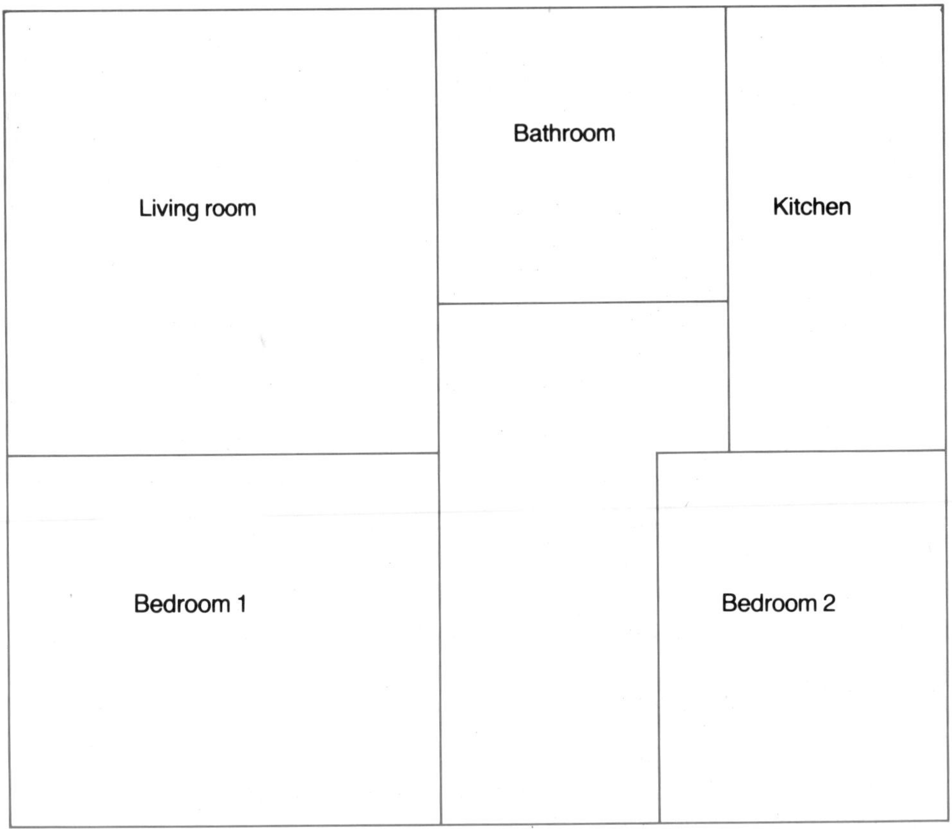

Fig. 26:2

| Room | Length (metres) | Width (metres) |
| --- | --- | --- |
| Bathroom | | |
| Living room | | |
| Kitchen | | |
| Bedroom 1 | | |
| Bedroom 2 | | |

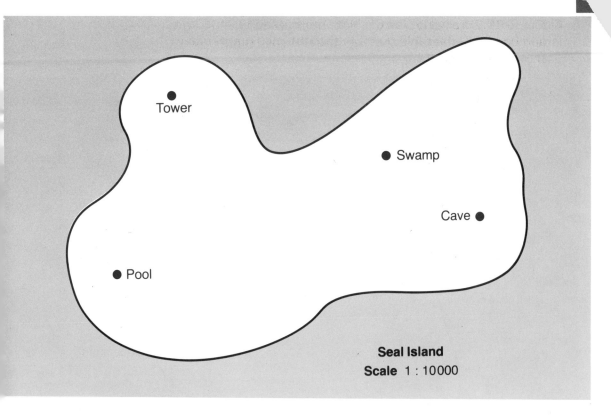

Tower

● Swamp

Cave ●

● Pool

**Seal Island**
**Scale** 1 : 10000

Fig. 26:3

**5** Figure 26:3 is a map of Seal Island.
1 cm on the map represents 100 m on the island.
There are 100 cm in 1 m.
So 100 m = 100 × 100 cm = 10 000 cm
The scale is 1 : 10 000.

Copy and complete the table. The first distance has been
calculated for you like this:
  From Pool to Tower on the map is 5 cm.
  5 cm on the map is 5 × 100 m = 500 m on the island

| From | To | Distance on map | Distance on island |
|------|------|------|------|
| Pool | Tower | 5 cm | 500 m |
| Pool | Swamp | | |
| Swamp | Tower | | |
| Cave | Swamp | | |
| Pool | Cave | | |

**6** Figure 26:4 is a map of Bronagh Island. Bronagh Island is larger than Seal Island in Figure 26:3, so the map maker has used a smaller scale. 1 cm represents 1 km.

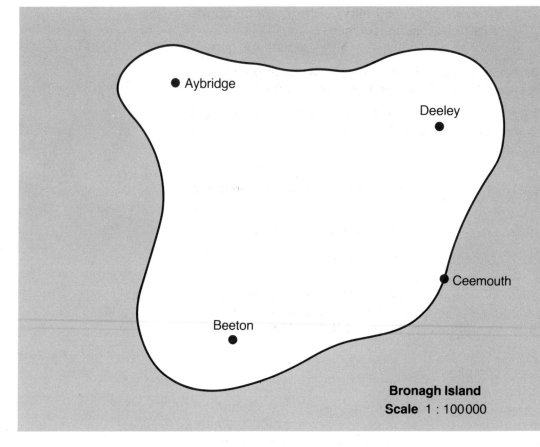

**Bronagh Island**
**Scale** 1 : 100 000

Fig. 26:4

There are 100 cm in 1 m. There are 1000 m in 1 km.
So 1 km = 1000 m = 100 000 cm.
The scale is 1 : 100 000.

Copy and complete the table.

| From | Distance | To |
|---|---|---|
| Beeton | 7 km | Aybridge |
| Beeton | 6 km | |
| Aybridge | 9 km | |
| Ceemouth | 4 km | |
| Deeley | 8 km | |

**7 Example** A model of a hospital is built to a scale of $1:60$. The model is 3 metres long. How long is the hospital?

The scale of $1:60$ tells us that 1 metre on the model represents 60 metres.
So the hospital is $3 \times 60 = 180$ metres long.

(a) A model bridge is 55 cm long. It has been built to the scale of $1:20$. How long is the real bridge?

(b) A swimming pool plan is 30 cm long. It has been drawn to the scale of $1:50$. How long is the pool  (i) in cm, (ii) in m?

**8** A model of a caravan is 25 cm long. The real caravan is 6 m long.

(a) How many centimetres long is the real caravan?

(b) What is the scale of the model?

**9** On a design for a rectangular kitchen unit, the unit top is 12 cm long and 4 cm wide. The actual unit is $1 \cdot 8$ m long and $0 \cdot 60$ m wide. What scale did the designer use?

**10** Copy and complete the table.

| Length | Measurement on plan | Scale | Actual measurement |
|---|---|---|---|
| Length of workshop | 4 cm | $1:100$ | m |
| Height of flagpole | 3 cm | $1:200$ | m |
| Width of radiator | 5 cm | $1:25$ | m |
| Gauge of railway | 9 cm | $1:16$ | m |

**11** Make a scale drawing of your classroom.

**12** Look at some Ordnance Survey maps, atlases, and maps in AA handbooks and geography books. Write about the different scales that are used.

**13** Do you or any of your friends make scale models? What scales have been used in making the models?

**14** Sometimes scales are used to magnify small objects so that they can be studied more easily. Find some drawings or photographs that are enlargements of small objects. You may find some in the books you use for other subjects such as science and history. Write about the scales that are used.

**15** Investigate scale copies made by a photocopier.

# A Finding journey distances

Sarah and Pauline set off from Exbourne and hike at a steady pace to Beaford and beyond. The clocks show their progress part of the way.

Fig. 27:1

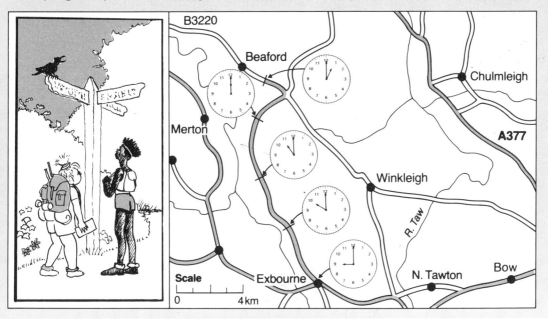

To answer questions 1 and 2 you need to know that Sarah and Pauline aim to hike at an average speed of 4 km/h.

1  How far from the starting point do they expect to be after:

(a)  1 hour      (b)  2 hours      (c)  3 hours      (d)  5 hours

(e)  7 hours      (f)  $\frac{1}{2}$ hour      (g)  $1\frac{1}{2}$ hours?

2  Sarah and Pauline set off at 9 o'clock. How far do they expect to have hiked by:

(a)  1 o'clock      (b)  3 o'clock?

3  Harvey expects to average 60 m.p.h. on a long motorway journey. How far does he expect to have travelled in:

(a)  2 hours      (b)  $\frac{1}{2}$ hour      (c)  $1\frac{1}{2}$ hours

(d)  a $\frac{1}{4}$ hour      (e)  $3\frac{1}{2}$ hours?

**4** Harvey got onto the motorway at 9:30 a.m. How far along the motorway does he expect to be by:

(a) 10:30 a.m. (b) noon (c) 9:45 a.m.

(d) 11:15 a.m.?

> Assume that his average speed is 60 m.p.h.

**5** Copy and complete the table.

| Speed of plane (km/h) | 600 | 600 | 600 | 600 | 600 | 600 | 600 | 600 |
|---|---|---|---|---|---|---|---|---|
| Time (h) | 1 | 2 | 3 | 4 | 5 | $\frac{1}{2}$ | $1\frac{1}{2}$ | $3\frac{1}{2}$ |
| Distance (km) | | | | | | | | |

**6** **Example** In the table shown in Figure 27:2 the distance from Sheffield to York is given as 52 miles.

| | SALISBURY | SHEFFIELD | SHREWSBURY | SOUTHAMPTON | STOKE | STRANRAER | TAUNTON | YORK |
|---|---|---|---|---|---|---|---|---|
| SHEFFIELD | 182 | | | | | | | |
| SHREWSBURY | 143 | 79 | | | | | | |
| SOUTHAMPTON | 23 | 192 | 163 | | | | | |
| STOKE | 155 | 47 | 34 | 170 | | | | |
| STRANRAER | 406 | 247 | 270 | 422 | 253 | | | |
| TAUNTON | 64 | 206 | 146 | 87 | 167 | 416 | | |
| YORK | 230 | 52 | 130 | 236 | 99 | 214 | 257 | |
| LONDON | 84 | 159 | 153 | 77 | 147 | 399 | 144 | 197 |

**Fig. 27:2**

How many miles is it from:

(a) Salisbury to York

(b) Stoke to Taunton

(c) Shrewsbury to Stranraer

(d) Stoke to Shrewsbury?

**7** Use the table in Figure 27:2 to find how far it is from:

(a) York to Stranraer

(b) Stranraer to Stoke

**8** (a) Walking at 90 m/min (a fast walking pace), how far do you go in 1 second?

(b) Allowing 4 seconds extra for safety, how long would it take you to cross a road 18 m wide?

(c) How many metres will a car travelling at 72 km/h cover in this time?

**9** Copy and complete this table for the crossing of a 16 m wide road:

| Speed of car (km/h) | 36 | 72 | 108 | 144 |
|---|---|---|---|---|
| Speed of car (m/s) | 10 | | | |
| Time to cross (s) | 13 | 13 | 13 | 13 |
| Distance covered by car (m) | 130 | | | |

**10** Figure 27:3 shows a graph drawn from the data in the table of question 9. Draw the graph on 2 mm graph paper, using scales of 1 cm to 10 km/h and 1 cm to 50 m. Read from the graph the minimum safe distance away that a car should be if you are to cross a 16 m wide road when the vehicle is travelling at:

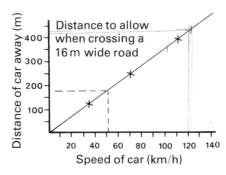

Fig. 27:3

(a) 50 km/h   (b) 100 km/h

(c) 120 km/h

**11** Illustrate the information of questions 9 and 10 on a full-size model marked out on your school field.

**12** Draw a chart to show the comparative average speeds of either different animals or different machines.

# B Finding journey times

## ▶ Points to discuss . . .

Figure 27:4 shows some journeys made by five sailors. Their speeds are given in knots (a knot is a speed of 1 nautical mile per hour). You can work out how far they travel by measuring and using the scale. When you know the distances and the speeds, you can work out how long each journey should take.

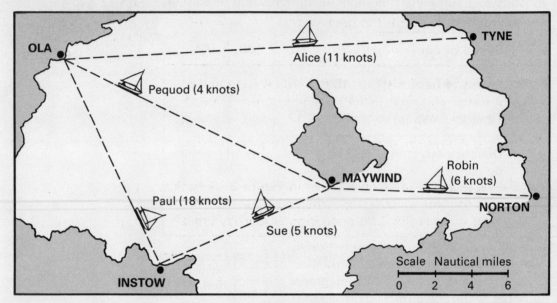

**Fig. 27:4**

**Example** Sue travels from Instow to Maywind, a map distance of 5 cm. From the scale, 1 cm represents 2 nautical miles, so 5 cm represents 10 nautical miles.

Sue travels 10 nautical miles at an average speed of 5 knots. This takes her 2 hours, because 10 ÷ 5 = 2.

**1** In Figure 27:4, find the total journey time for:

(a) Alice    (b) Pequod    (c) Paul    (d) Robin

(e) Sue, if she travels directly from Instow to Norton at 5 knots

**2** Clarke's hiking group decide to walk around the blue route. They know they usually manage to average about 4 km/h.

'12 km at 4 km/h will take us 3 hours,' says Petra.

'Yes, because 12 ÷ 4 = 3,' agrees Rhani.

Find how long the group should take to walk:

(a) the red route     (b) the green route

(c) the orange route

Fig. 27:5

---

**3** Look at Figure 27:4. On the return journey, Pequod takes Paul's route, and Paul takes Pequod's route. They still travel at their original speeds.

Work out the return journey times for Pequod and Paul.

**4** If the fastest and the slowest ship in Figure 27:4 both leave Ola for Tyne at 9:00 p.m., when does each arrive at Tyne, and what is the difference in their journey times?

# C Finding average speeds

## ▶ Points to discuss . . .

Figure 27:6 shows a map of Tranquility Island, a signpost at the bus depot, and four bus journey times.

| Bus Journey Times | |
|---|---|
| Around coast | 3 hr |
| Mt Breathless (out) | 1½ hr |
| Mt Breathless (return) | 1 hr |
| Sandstorm bay | 1½ hr |

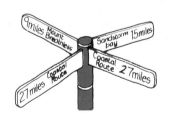

Fig. 27:6

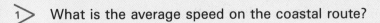

1▷ What is the average speed on the coastal route?

2▷ What is the average speed of the bus to Mt Breathless?

3 ▷ What is the average speed of the bus from Mt Breathless back to the depot?

4 ▷ What is the average speed of the bus to Sandstorm Bay?

**1** Find the average speed of these joggers.

(a) Prudence, who covers 16 miles in 4 hours

(b) Sue, who covers 20 miles in 4 hours

(c) François, who covers 30 kilometres in 6 hours

(d) Leila, who covers 18 kilometres in 4 hours

| Average speed (km/h) | 30 | 30 | 45 | 30 | 20 | 30 | 20 | 15 | (i) | (j) | (k) | (l) |
|---|---|---|---|---|---|---|---|---|---|---|---|---|
| Time          (hours) | 1 | 2 | 1 | 3 | (e) | (f) | (g) | (h) | 1 | 1 | 2 | 10 |
| Distance      (km) | (a) | (b) | (c) | (d) | 20 | 30 | 40 | 30 | 25 | 40 | 40 | 50 |

**3** What is my average speed if I go:

(a) 200 km in 4 h     (b) 175 miles in 7 h?

**4** A train travels 25 miles. What is its average speed if it takes:

(a) 1 h     (b) 2 h     (c) $\frac{1}{2}$ h     (d) $\frac{1}{4}$ h     (e) 20 min?

**5** If Rob drives his cement lorry into town early in the morning he usually covers the 90 miles in 2 hours.
On the return journey he is often caught in traffic, and takes about 3 hours.

What are his two average speeds?

**6** Figure 27:7 shows a steamer trip on the River Arrow. Becky prefers maths to river banks, so she spends the journey keeping a record of the average speed of the boat on the trip. Copy and complete her table.

Fig. 27:7

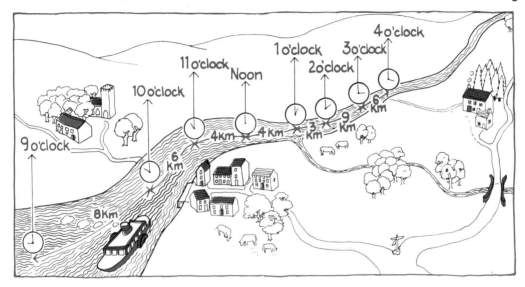

| Time taken (hours) | Total distance travelled in that time (km) | Average speed up to this point in the journey (km/hour) |
|---|---|---|
| 1 | 8 | 8 |
| 2 | 14 | e |
| 3 | 18 | f |
| 4 | a | g |
| 5 | b | h |
| 6 | c | i |
| 7 | d | j |

Fig. 27:8

**7** In 1985 in the London Marathon, Ingrid Christiansen ran the 26·2188 miles in 2·3502 hours. Use your calculator to find her average speed. This is the fastest time to date ever achieved by a woman in the marathon. Find out about this year's marathon (it is normally run at Easter time). Who won and at what average speed?

Are your answers sensible? How accurately can we measure time? What about speed?

# A Pictograms

Figure 28:1 is called a **pictogram**. Each picture represents one pupil.

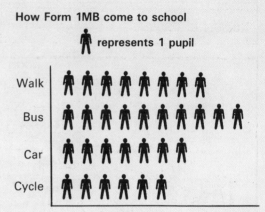

How Form 1MB come to school

represents 1 pupil

Walk
Bus
Car
Cycle

Fig. 28:1

**1** Copy and complete the pictogram shown in Figure 28:2, using the data (or information) in this table.

| Car colour | Red | Blue | Green | White | Yellow |
|---|---|---|---|---|---|
| Number of cars | 50 | 20 | 14 | 18 | 11 |

**Car colour survey by Form 1MB**

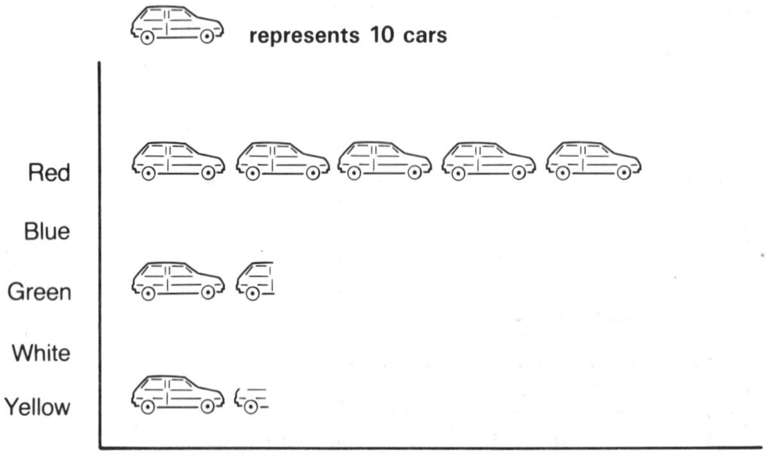

 represents 10 cars

Red
Blue
Green
White
Yellow

Fig. 28:2

**2** Jeanne conducts a survey of her class, class 1MB, to find their favourite type of book. Draw a pictogram to illustrate her data.

| Type of book | Western | Adventure | Animal | Science Fiction | Travel |
|---|---|---|---|---|---|
| Number of votes | 4 | 7 | 8 | 8 | 3 |

**3** Ask all of the members of your class how they came to school. Illustrate your findings with a pictogram.

# B Bar-charts

Figure 28:3 is called a **bar-chart**. The bars can be horizontal or vertical.

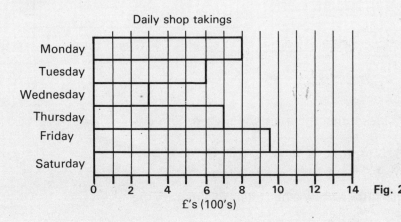

Daily shop takings

Fig. 28:3

1 Copy and complete the bar-chart shown in Figure 28:4 for the following data.

Rainfall in centimetres in Rio de Janeiro

| Rainfall (cm) | 11 | 11 | 12 | 10 | $7\frac{1}{2}$ | 5 | 4 | $4\frac{1}{2}$ | 6 | $7\frac{1}{2}$ | 10 | 13 |
|---|---|---|---|---|---|---|---|---|---|---|---|---|
| Month | J | F | M | A | M | J | J | A | S | O | N | D |

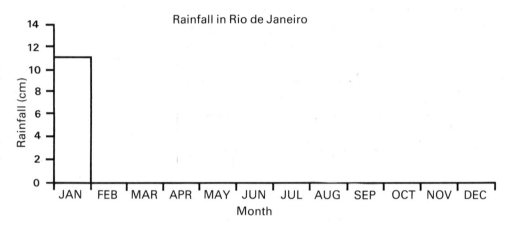

Fig. 28:4

2 Copy the tally-chart and complete the totals column. Then draw a bar-chart, numbered from 0 to 10, to illustrate the data.

| | Tally | Totals |
|---|---|---|
| Walk | LHT    /// | 8 |
| Bus | LHT    LHT | |
| Car | LHT    // | |
| Cycle | LHT | |
| | Grand total | 30 |

3 Shelley asks her classmates for their shoe sizes. She collects the data:
4, 6, 6, 4, 7, 6, 5, 5, 4, 6, 7, 8, 4, 6, 5, 6, 5, 5, 6, 7, 4, 7, 5, 6, 4, 7, 5, 5, 7, 5

Draw up a tally-chart, then draw a bar-chart to illustrate the data.

**4** Draw up a tally-chart, then draw a bar-chart, for the following data, which gives the amounts (in pence) spent by pupils at a school tuck-shop.

8, 7, 5, 6, 10, 12, 6, 7, 10, 5, 9, 4, 3, 8, 11, 7, 7, 5, 8, 7, 4, 7, 4, 7, 6, 9, 8, 12, 11, 7, 7, 5, 8, 8, 4, 9, 10, 3, 5, 5

**5**

| Letter | Tally | Totals |
|---|---|---|
| A | | |
| B | | |
| C | | |
| D | | |
| E | | |
| and so on | | |
| Z | | |

Choose a page in any book. Make a tally-chart to show how many times each letter appears. Stop when the letter with most appearances reaches 100.

Draw a bar-chart to illustrate your findings and compare your results with those of other members of your class.

# C Line graphs

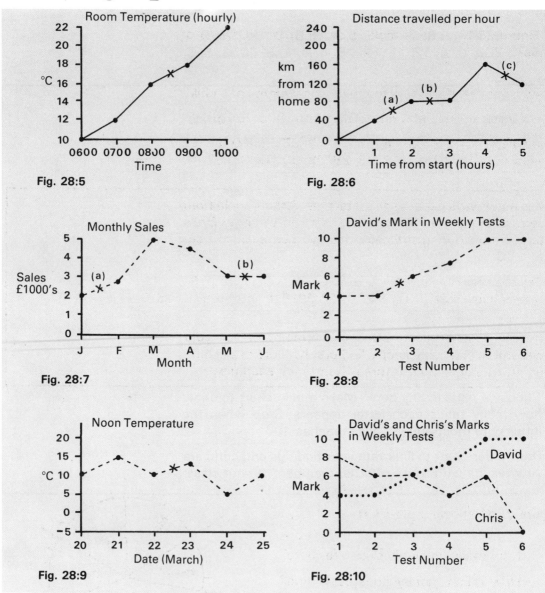

Fig. 28:5

Fig. 28:6

Fig. 28:7

Fig. 28:8

Fig. 28:9

Fig. 28:10

**1** In Figure 28:5, at what time was the room temperature 18 °C?

**2** In Figure 28:6, at what two times was the distance from home the same?

**3** In Figure 28:8, the point marked X has no meaning. Why?

**4** In Figure 28:8, would David's teacher be pleased with him? Why?

**5** In Figure 28:9, is the temperature on 26 March likely to be: below 5 °C,   between 5 °C and 15 °C,   above 15 °C?

**6** In Figure 28:10, who is making better progress, David or Chris?

**7** Draw a line graph to show the following weights of a child.

Use a vertical scale of 1 cm to 5 kg from 0 to 40 kg.

| Age (years) | 1 | 2 | 3 | 4 | 5 | 6 | 7 | 8 | 9 | 10 | 11 | 12 |
|---|---|---|---|---|---|---|---|---|---|---|---|---|
| Weight (kg) | 10 | 13 | 17 | 19 | 23 | 26 | 28 | 30 | 33 | 35 | 37 | 40 |

---

**8** It is not always necessary to start the vertical scale from zero. Beginning at 35 °C, draw a graph to show Eva's temperature during an illness. Use a vertical scale of 1 cm to 1 °C.

| Day of illness | 1 | 2 | 3 | 4 | 5 | 6 | 7 | 8 | 9 | 10 |
|---|---|---|---|---|---|---|---|---|---|---|
| Temperature (°C) | 37 | 37·2 | 37·8 | 38 | 39·6 | 40 | 40 | 39 | 37·2 | 36·9 |

**9** If your teacher can obtain a thermometer for your classroom you could keep a line-graph record of the temperature, say at two or three fixed times each day.

---

# D Pie-charts

▶ **Points to discuss . . .**

Figure 28:11 shows a **pie-chart**.

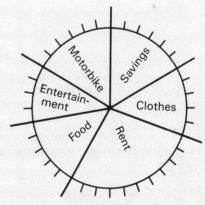

**Fig. 28:11**     **How Ian spent £36**

1▷ How many small divisions are there?

2▷ How much money does each small division represent?

3▷ How much did Ian spend on each item?

4▷ How many degrees wide is each small division?

5▷ How many degrees are there for each item?

**1** Eight children were asked about their favourite flavour ice-cream. Figure 28:12 is a pie-chart showing how they answered.

(a) Which flavour is the most popular?

(b) What fraction of the children chose the most popular flavour?

(c) How many prefer vanilla?

(d) How many prefer chocolate?

(e) How many prefer strawberry?

Fig. 28:12

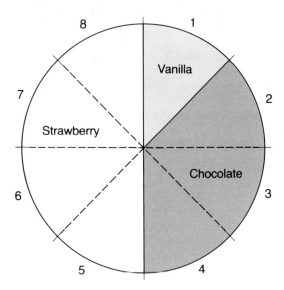

Favourite ice-cream flavours

**2** One evening Tracy was asked what she had done in the past twelve hours. The pie-chart in Figure 28:13 shows how she spent her time.

(a) What activity lasted five hours?

(b) How long did Tracy take to do her homework?

(c) What activity took a quarter of the twelve hours?

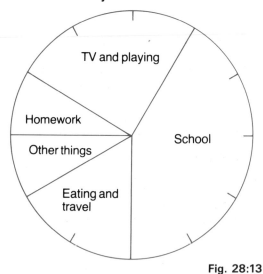

12 hours in Tracy's life

Fig. 28:13

**3** (a) How many degrees are there in a complete circle?

(b) If a pie-chart is divided into 36 equal parts, how many degrees at the centre of each part?

(c) Use a circle divided into 36 equal parts to draw a pie-chart that shows the results of a survey of 36 shoppers asked to say what was their favourite cake mix.

Riso 10; Quickbake 3; Mrs Bod's 12; Yuk 3; Egad 8

**4** Eighteen children were asked about their holidays. The pie-chart in Figure 28:14 shows how they replied.

(a) How many stayed at home?

(b) Which was more popular, London or abroad?

(c) How many more went to the seaside than to the country?

(d) What fraction stayed at home?

(e) What fraction went abroad?

**Where we go on holiday**

Fig. 28:14

**5** Ask 36 pupils in your year about their pets. They must answer in one of the following groups:

**A** Only a dog     **B** Only a cat     **C** Only a bird
**D** More than one pet     **E** No pets

Draw a pie-chart to illustrate the result of your survey.

**6** There are 18 cars parked in a car park. Six are grey, two are black, four are red, one is white, and five are green. Draw a pie-chart to illustrate this.

**7** Mr Maguz has a new garden in which he plants some fruit trees. Twelve are apple trees, two are pear trees, three are plum trees, and one is a cherry tree. Draw a pie-chart to illustrate this.

**8** Collect statistical charts from newspapers and magazines. Write about them saying what kind of graphs they are, and how clearly and honestly they represent the data.

# Using fractions

# A Fractions of many

▶ **Points to discuss . . .**

1 ▷ When we talk of 'a class of pupils', how many pupils might that be? How many pupils might there be in half a class?

2 ▷ When we talk about 'a whole turn', how many degrees do we turn through? How many degrees would we turn through in $\frac{1}{2}$ a turn? How many degrees in $\frac{1}{3}$ of a turn?

3 ▷ Look at this table which Stanislav has written. What do you notice about all the numbers in the Number column? What would happen if Stanislav had used odd numbers? What other things might Stanislav have put in his table?

| | Number | ½ as many |
|---|---|---|
| A box of matches. | 52 | 26 |
| My tutor group. | 26 | 13 |
| Hockey team and reserve. | 12 | 6 |
| Photos on a camera film. | 24 | 12 |

Fig. 29:1

● **To remind you . . .**

- $\frac{3}{4}$ is a **common fraction**.

- The **denominator** (to denominate is to name something) is the bottom number. The denominator tells us into how many equal pieces the complete amount is to be divided.

- The **numerator** (to numerate is to count) is the top number. The numerator tells us how many of the equal pieces make up the complete fraction.

- A **top-heavy fraction**, like $\frac{11}{5}$, is called an 'improper fraction'.

- A **mixed number** is partly a whole number and partly a common fraction, like $7\frac{1}{4}$.

- **Equivalent** fractions are the same amount of the whole thing, for instance $\frac{3}{6}$ and $\frac{4}{8}$ are both equivalent to $\frac{1}{2}$.

**1** Three out of five pens have blue ink. What fraction do not have blue ink?

**2** Look at the bar of chocolate. It may help you to answer these questions.

(a) Which is larger, $\frac{1}{2}$ or $\frac{7}{12}$?

(b) Which is smaller, $\frac{5}{12}$ or $\frac{1}{3}$?

Fig. 29:2

**3** There are 28 pupils in a class. 17 are girls. What fraction of the class are boys?

**4** There are 21 girls and 24 boys in a youth club. What fraction of the youth club are girls?

**5** A farmer has 24 animals. There are 8 cows, 6 pigs, 3 horses, and some turkeys. What fraction of his animals is each kind? Write your fraction in its simplest form.

**6** In an orchard there are 20 apple trees, 18 pear trees, 12 plum trees, and 10 cherry trees. What fraction of the orchard is:

(a) apple trees    (b) cherry trees

(c) apple trees and plum trees    (d) not plum trees?

**7** This bar of chocolate will break into 24 equal pieces. Twenty-four girls could have one piece each. What other number of girls could share the chocolate pieces equally? (There are five possible answers.)

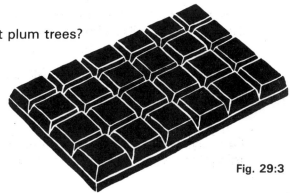

Fig. 29:3

**8** For each number of girls in your answers to question 7, what fraction of the bar does each girl receive?

**9** Krystal counted 6 members of her class wearing spectacles. There are 30 pupils in her class. Figure 29:4 shows the diagram that Krystal drew.

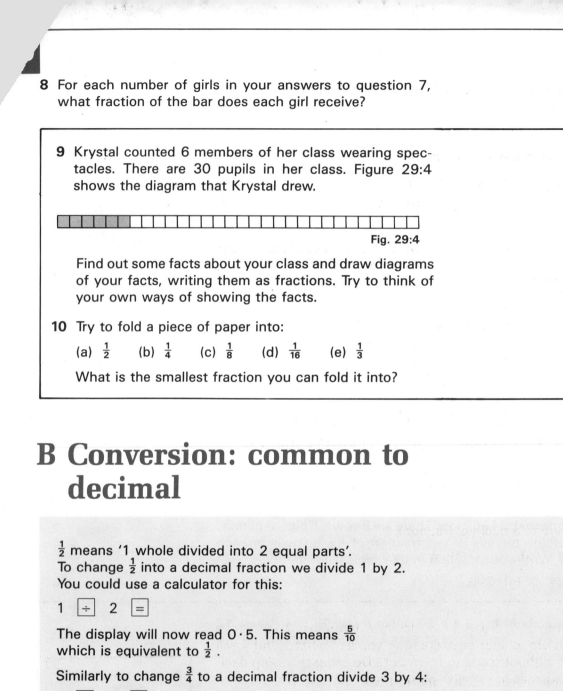

Fig. 29:4

Find out some facts about your class and draw diagrams of your facts, writing them as fractions. Try to think of your own ways of showing the facts.

**10** Try to fold a piece of paper into:

(a) $\frac{1}{2}$   (b) $\frac{1}{4}$   (c) $\frac{1}{8}$   (d) $\frac{1}{16}$   (e) $\frac{1}{3}$

What is the smallest fraction you can fold it into?

# B Conversion: common to decimal

$\frac{1}{2}$ means '1 whole divided into 2 equal parts'.
To change $\frac{1}{2}$ into a decimal fraction we divide 1 by 2.
You could use a calculator for this:

1 ÷ 2 =

The display will now read 0·5. This means $\frac{5}{10}$ which is equivalent to $\frac{1}{2}$.

Similarly to change $\frac{3}{4}$ to a decimal fraction divide 3 by 4:

3 ÷ 4 =

The display will now read 0·75. This means $\frac{75}{100}$ which is equivalent to $\frac{3}{4}$.

**1** Change to a decimal fraction:

(a) $\frac{1}{2}$   (b) $\frac{1}{4}$   (c) $\frac{3}{8}$   (d) $\frac{7}{10}$   (e) $\frac{7}{100}$   (f) $\frac{1}{5}$

(g) $\frac{4}{5}$   (h) $\frac{1}{10}$   (i) $\frac{1}{100}$

**2** When changing a mixed number to a decimal fraction, the whole number part is unchanged.

**Example** $3\frac{3}{4} \rightarrow 3\cdot75$

Change to a decimal number:

(a) $1\frac{3}{4}$    (b) $6\frac{1}{4}$    (c) $5\frac{1}{8}$

(d) $11\frac{9}{10}$    (e) $10\frac{65}{100}$    (f) $3\frac{33}{100}$

**3** Many fractions do not change to exact decimals. Instead they 'recur', that is they start to repeat. We show the repeated figures by placing a dot over them.

**Examples**    $0\cdot3333333 \ldots \rightarrow 0\cdot\dot3$
                $0\cdot4666666 \ldots \rightarrow 0\cdot4\dot6$
                $6\cdot415415415 \ldots \rightarrow 6\cdot\dot41\dot5$

Write the following using recurrence dots.

(a) $0\cdot444444444$     (b) $0\cdot99999999999$

(c) $0\cdot73333333333$     (d) $0\cdot3434343434$

(e) $0\cdot314314314314$     (f) $0\cdot503095030950309$

**4** Divide by 9 each number from 1 to 9.

**5** Change to a decimal fraction:

(a) $\frac{2}{3}$    (b) $\frac{1}{6}$    (c) $\frac{1}{15}$    (d) $\frac{11}{15}$    (e) $\frac{2}{17}$

(f) $2\frac{3}{8}$    (g) $3\frac{3}{100}$

**6** Write $\frac{1}{7}$, $\frac{2}{7}$, $\frac{3}{7}$ and $\frac{4}{7}$ as decimal fractions. Look for a pattern in your answers. Can you say what $\frac{5}{7}$ and $\frac{6}{7}$ will be without working them out? Do other recurring decimals follow a similar pattern ($\frac{1}{9}$s; $\frac{1}{11}$s; $\frac{1}{13}$s; $\frac{1}{17}$s; etc.)?

**7** Mathematicians have known for a long time that no matter what size circle is drawn its circumference is always 'three and a bit' times longer than its diameter. The number 'three and a bit' is represented by the Greek letter $\pi$ (pronounced 'pi').

Over the centuries different mathematicians have suggested various values for $\pi$. Some are shown here. What are their decimal equivalents?

Babylonian (500 BC) $3\frac{1}{8}$

Greek (220 BC) $\frac{211\,875}{67\,441}$

Chinese (AD 500) $\frac{355}{113}$

Greek (AD 200) $\frac{377}{120}$

Indian (AD 400) $\frac{3927}{1250}$

Use your library to look for more suggested values for $\pi$.

# C Conversion: decimal to common

To convert from a decimal fraction to a common fraction you have to think about the column heading of the last figure.

| 10s | 1s | $\frac{1}{10}$s | $\frac{1}{100}$s | $\frac{1}{1000}$s |
|-----|-----|-----|-----|-----|
|     |     |     |     |     |

**Example**  Change 0·3 to a common fraction.

The 3 is in the $\frac{1}{10}$s column.

0·3 is $\frac{3}{10}$.

Note: Some people think that $\frac{1}{3}$ is 0·3.
$\frac{1}{3}$ is not 0·3, but 0·333333333 . . .

**Example**  Change 0·43 to a common fraction.

The 3 is in the $\frac{1}{100}$s column.
0·43 is $\frac{43}{100}$.

**Example**  Change 9·125 to a mixed number.

The 5 is in the $\frac{1}{1000}$s column.
9·125 is $9\frac{125}{1000}$.
$\frac{125}{1000}$ will cancel:

$$\frac{125}{1000} \xrightarrow{\text{divide both by 5}} \frac{25}{200} \xrightarrow{\text{divide both by 5}} \frac{5}{40}$$

$$\frac{5}{40} \xrightarrow{\text{divide both by 5}} \frac{1}{8}$$

Answer: 9·125 is $9\frac{1}{8}$.

1  Write as a common fraction:

(a)  0·7      (b)  0·9      (c)  0·11      (d)  0·37

(e)  0·121      (f)  0·07      (g)  0·009      (h)  0·067

(i)  0·03      (j)  0·0001

2 Write as a common fraction:

(a) 0·3      (b) 0·1      (c) 0·31      (d) 0·129

(e) 0·041      (f) 0·09      (g) 0·007      (h) 0·13

(i) 0·0003      (j) 0·0081

3 If possible we simplify the fractions by cancelling.

Note that all multiples of ten will only divide by multiples of 2 and 5, so only even numbers and numbers ending in 5 will cancel in these questions.

The cancelling is usually written as in Figure 29:5.

*Sam cancelled this way.*

**Fig. 29:5**

*Can you think of a quicker way?*

Write as a simplified common fraction:

(a) 0·5      (b) 0·8      (c) 0·25

(d) 0·04      (e) 0·15      (f) 0·35

4 Write as a mixed number in its simplest form:

(a) 3·4      (b) 7·8      (c) 5·6      (d) 2·15

(e) 4·55

5 Example   In Figure 29:6 the arrow is pointing to 6·4, or $6\frac{4}{10}$ which simplifies to $6\frac{2}{5}$.

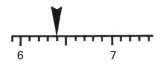

To what number is each arrow pointing in Figure 29:7? Give your answer as a decimal and as a mixed number.

(a)
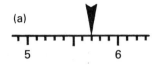

(b)

(c)

(d)

**Fig. 29:7**

**6 Example** In Figure 29:8, the arrow is pointing to $2\frac{5}{8}$.

$\frac{5}{8} \rightarrow 5 \div 8 = 0 \cdot 625$, so the arrow is pointing to $2 \cdot 625$.

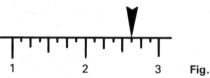

**Fig. 29:8**

To what number is each arrow pointing in Figure 29:9? Give your answer as a mixed number and as a decimal.

(a)

(b)

(c)
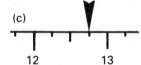

(d)
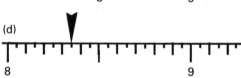

**Fig. 29:9**

---

**7** Draw some number lines of your own. Put an arrow over your lines and write the value as a mixed number and as a decimal fraction.

# Summaries

## 1 Networks

Figure S1 shows a network. It has five nodes (shown by ●), seven arcs (lines joining nodes), and four regions (remember the outside).

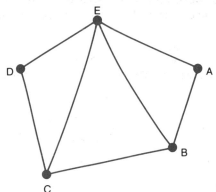

Fig. S1

A, D and E have an even number of arcs leaving them and are even nodes.

This network can be drawn without repeating a line or taking your pencil off the paper – it is traversable. If a network has more than two odd nodes it is not traversable.

## 2 Integers: addition and subtraction

Integers are whole numbers like 1, 12, 156, 0.

You should know how to add (find the sum) and subtract (find the difference) and **when** to add and subtract.

Always think about your answer – is it sensible?

## 4 Angles: the protractor; kinds of angle

There are 360° in a complete turn.

We measure angles in degrees with a protractor.

## 5 Decimals: addition and subtraction

The decimal point separates the whole numbers from the fractions of numbers.

100s   10s   1s $\cdot \frac{1}{10}$s   $\frac{1}{100}$s   $\frac{1}{1000}$s

You should know how to add and subtract decimals and **when** to add and subtract. It is easier when you put the decimals in columns.

**Example**   $3\cdot4 + 1\cdot95$

$$
\begin{array}{r}
3\cdot4 \\
+\ 1\cdot95 \\
\hline
5\cdot35 \\
\hline
\end{array}
$$

It is helpful to use zeros as 'space fillers'.

**Example**   $3\cdot4 - 1\cdot95$

$$
\begin{array}{r}
3\cdot40 \\
-\ 1\cdot95 \\
\hline
1\cdot45 \\
\hline
\end{array}
$$

You should know
- how to write decimals
- how to say decimals
- what decimals mean.

# 6   Circles: naming parts

The circumference is the perimeter (all the way around) of a circle.
An arc is part of the circumference.
A semi-circle is half of a circle when it is divided by a diameter.

diameter = 2 × radius

# 7   Metric system: length

The basic unit of length in the metric system is the metre.
Metre is written m for short.

Other units of length are millimetre (mm), centimetre (cm) and kilometre (km).

- milli means $\frac{1}{1000}$ so a millimetre is $\frac{1}{1000}$ part of a metre
- centi means $\frac{1}{100}$ so a centimetre is $\frac{1}{100}$ part of a metre
- kilo means 1000, so a kilometre is 1000 metres.

A door is about 2 m tall. A new pencil is about 15 cm long. A pin head is about 1 mm.

# 8   Multiplication of integers and decimals

Multiplication is a quick way to add lots of the same number.
Instead of $3 + 3 + 3 + 3 + 3 = 15$ you can use $5 \times 3 = 15$.

The answer to a multiplication is called the product. The product of 5 and 7 is 35.

Most people think it is important that you can multiply any digit by any digit in your head.

You should know that 4 × 7 is the same as 7 × 4.

When you find multiplications such as 27 × 23, you can write:

```
    27
×   23
    81   This is 27 × 3.
+  540   This is 27 × 20.
   621   This is 27 × 23.
```

Multiplying by 10 moves the figures one column to the left making them worth ten times as much.

| 100 | 10 | 1 | $\frac{1}{10}$ | $\frac{1}{100}$ | |
|---|---|---|---|---|---|
| | | 0 • 7 | | | 0·7 |
| | | 7 • | | | 0·7 × 10 |

Always make sure your answers are sensible. You should have some idea of the answer by using an approximation.

**Example**   28 × 22 is about 30 × 20.
30 × 20 = 600.
28 × 22 is about 600 (28 × 22 = 616).

# 9   Polygons: names

A polygon is a flat (plane) shape with any number of straight sides.

Some special polygons (with their number of sides in brackets) are: triangle (3), quadrilateral (4), pentagon (5), hexagon (6), octagon (8), decagon (10).

A regular polygon has all its sides equal and all its angles equal.

# 10   Integers: division

Division is sharing into equal amounts. There are many ways to say and write what we mean by division.

8 shared into 2 equal parts        8 divided by 2

8 ÷ 2        2)8        $\frac{8}{2}$

When 9 apples are shared equally between 2 people, each

person will have 4 apples and there will be a remainder of 1 apple. This can be written $9 \div 2 = 4\,r\,1$

The remainder can also be written as a fraction. The remainder of 1 becomes $\frac{1}{2}$ when we divide 1 by 2.
$$9 \div 2 = 4\tfrac{1}{2}$$
We can check this by multiplying the answer by 2.
$$4\tfrac{1}{2} \times 2 = 9$$

When we use a calculator to divide the remainder is shown as a decimal
$$9 \div 2 = 4 \cdot 5$$
$4 \cdot 5$ is 4 units and 5 tenths or $4\tfrac{5}{10}$, which is $4\tfrac{1}{2}$. We can check this by multiplying the answer by 2.
$$4 \cdot 5 \times 2 = 9$$

It is a good idea to check your divisions by multiplying.

# 11 Graphs: coordinates

The $x$-coordinate is written first. See *coordinate* in the glossary.

# 12 Tessellations

Tessellations are tiling patterns which cover a surface without leaving any gaps.

Congruent shapes are the same shape and size.

# 13 Area: rectangles

A measure of the amount of surface.
Units commonly used are $cm^2$ (square centimetres), $m^2$ (square metre), and $km^2$ (square kilometre).

Area of rectangle = length $\times$ width square units.

# 14 Common fractions: fractions of a whole

A quarter ($\frac{1}{4}$) is called a common fraction.

Equivalent fractions are all the same fraction written in a different way like $\frac{2}{4} = \frac{1}{2}$.

Fractions should be written as simply as possible by cancelling. Cancelling is dividing the top and bottom numbers by the same number. Cancelling does not change the value of the fraction.

The mixed number $1\frac{3}{4}$ is equivalent to the 'top-heavy' fraction $\frac{7}{4}$ because $1\frac{3}{4} = \frac{4}{4} + \frac{3}{4} = \frac{7}{4}$.

When we write a half as $0 \cdot 5$ we call it a decimal fraction, often just called a decimal.

# 15  Metric measure: weight, capacity

## Weight

The basic unit is the kilogram (kg) which is about $2\frac{1}{4}$ lb. The gram (g) is a very small weight, about the weight of two drawing pins.

1 kg = 1000 g, the weight of a standard bag of sugar.

1 tonne = 1000 kg, about the weight of a large family car.

To change kg to g, multiply by 1000.
To change g to kg, divide by 1000.

## Capacity

When we measure the volume of a container used for liquids or gases we talk of its capacity.

The basic unit is the litre which is about $1\frac{3}{4}$ pints.
1 litre = 100 centilitres (cl) = 1000 millilitres (ml)

To change litres to millilitres, multiply by 1000.
To change litres to centilitres, multiply by 100.
To change millilitres to litres, divide by 1000.

# 16, 17  Reflection

O is an object. I is its image.

The line OI crosses the mirror line at right-angles at M.
The distances OM and MI are equal.
The image is the same distance behind the mirror as the object is in front of it.

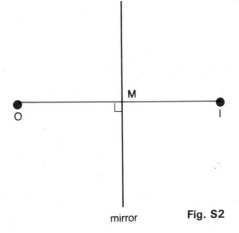

mirror          Fig. S2

# 18  Symmetry: line

Symmetrical shapes are 'balanced' on either side of their line (or axis) of symmetry – their 'fold' line or 'mirror' line.

Some shapes have no lines of symmetry. Some have one line of symmetry. Others have more than one line of symmetry.

A symmetrical shape folds in half along any line of symmetry.

# 19 Triangles: types, angle sum

For the types of triangle, see Figures 19:1 to 19:6 (page 132).

The three angles of a triangle add up to 180°. This is called the angle-sum of the triangle.

# 20 Percentages: % ↔ fraction

Per cent (%) means 'out of 100', so 99% means 99 out of $100 = \frac{99}{100}$

**Changing a fraction to a percentage**
You should know $\frac{1}{4} = 25\%$, $\frac{1}{2} = 50\%$, $\frac{3}{4} = 75\%$, whole = 100%

To change other fractions, multiply them by 100%.

**Example** $\frac{2}{5}$ as a percentage is $\frac{2}{5} \times 100\% = 40\%$
$0 \cdot 6$ as a percentage is $0 \cdot 6 \times 100\% = 60\%$

You should know
   25% of £1 = 25p
   50% of £1 = 50p
   100% of £1 = 100p or £1
and any percentage of £1 like
   32% of £1 = 32p
   1% of £1 = 1p

# 21 Time: units; clocks; calendar

**Units**   1 hour = 60 minutes, 1 minute = 60 seconds
   24 hours = 1 day, 365 days = 1 year
   7 days = 1 week, 52 weeks = 1 year

To change hours to minutes, multiply by 60.
To change minutes to hours, divide by 60.

# 22 Approximations: rounding

Approximate means 'roughly the same as'. We use approximations very often in our lives, particularly when we talk about numbers

124 to the nearest 10 is 120 (124 is nearer to 120 than 130).
128 to the nearest 10 is 130 (128 is nearer to 130 than 120).
125 to the nearest 10 is 130 (when it is exactly halfway we round up).
75p to the nearest £ is £1.
£3·94 to the nearest £ is £4.

# 23 Decimal fractions: division by 10, 100, 1000

To divide by 10, move the figures one column to the right (that makes them worth a tenth as much). Write a zero when there is nothing in the units column.

**Example**  $3·2 \div 10 = 0·32$

To divide by 100, move the figures two columns to the right (this makes them worth a hundredth as much).

**Example**  $3·2 \div 100 = 0·032$

To divide by 1000, move the figures three columns to the right (this makes them worth a thousandth as much).

**Example**  $3·2 \div 1000 = 0·0032$

You should know how to divide money by 10, 100 and 1000.

**Examples**  $£24·00 \div 10 = £2·40$
$£35·00 \div 100 = £0·35$
$£850·00 \div 1000 = £0·85$

# 24 Statistics: the mean

The mean is a number which represents a set of numbers. The mean is usually just called 'the average'. It is found by dividing the total of all the items by the number of items.

**Example**  The mean (average) of £2, £2, £3, £5 is

$$\frac{£2 + £2 + £3 + £5}{4} = \frac{£12}{4} = £3$$

# 25 Integers: kinds of integers

An integer is a whole number like 5, 17, 0, 118.

Rectangular numbers can be shown as a rectangle of dots or a square of dots.

**Example**
• • • •
• • • •

Square numbers can be shown as a square of dots.

**Example**
• • •
• • •
• • •

All square numbers, except 1, are also rectangular numbers.

Triangular numbers can be shown as a triangle of dots.

**Example**
•
• •
• • •

Factors divide exactly into a number.

**Example**  The factors of 12 are 1, 2, 3, 4, 6 and 12.
You can check whether you have all the factors by multiplying pairs of numbers to make 12.

1    2    3    4    6    12

*What if it is a square number?*

# 26  Scales: scale drawing

A scale drawing may have a scale of 1 : 100. We read this as 'one to a hundred'. It means that 1 unit on the drawing represents 100 of the same units on the object.

**Example**  A patio 10 m by 6 m would be drawn 10 cm by 6 cm using a 1 : 100 scale.

# 27  Time; distance; speed

**Distance**

The basic unit is the metre (m). The metre is too small for everyday travel and so the kilometre is used in many countries.

1 km = 1000 metres

The mile is used to measure large distances in the United Kingdom. It is larger than the kilometre.
1 mile is about 1·6 km.

**Speed**

$$\text{Speed} = \frac{\text{distance}}{\text{time}} \text{ (for example, 30 m.p.h.)}$$

$$\text{Average speed} = \frac{\text{total distance travelled}}{\text{total time taken}}$$

# 28  Statistics: charts

Charts give information in diagram form. Types of charts are

- pictograms (Figure 28:1, page 196)
- bar-charts (Figure 28:3, page 197)
- line graphs (Figures 28:5 to 28:10, page 200)
- pie-charts (Figure 28:11, page 201)

# 29  Using fractions

To change $\frac{3}{4}$ to a decimal fraction, divide 3 by 4. Using a calculator, press  3  $\boxed{\div}$  4  $\boxed{=}$ . The display is $0 \cdot 75$, which means $\frac{75}{100}$ – this is equivalent to $\frac{3}{4}$.

To change $0 \cdot 6$ to a common fraction, rewrite it as $\frac{6}{10}$ (because the 6 is in the tenths column). You can cancel $\frac{6}{10}$ to $\frac{3}{5}$, so $0 \cdot 6 = \frac{3}{5}$.

Words in *italic* can be looked up in this glossary.

## A

### Acute angle
An angle which measures greater than 0° but less than 90°.

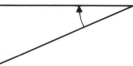

### Angle
A measure of the amount of turn. There are four kinds of angle, e.g. *acute angle, obtuse angle, reflex angle, right-angle*.

### Angle-sum
If we add the measure of angles together they form an angle-sum. The angle-sum of a triangle is 180°. $a + b + c = 180°$

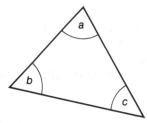

### Anti-clockwise
Going in the opposite direction to the hands of a clock.

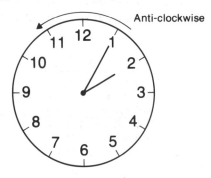

### Approximate
Means 'not exactly'. Because no measurement can be exact, all units of measure are approximate. Any number that is not exact, but has been rounded off to several decimal places, is called an **approximation**. See also *rounding*.

### Arc
A part of a curve. Usually we are referring to part of the *circumference* of a circle.

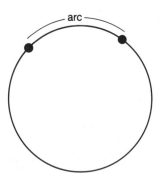

A line joining *nodes* in a *network* (e.g. the line joining A to B) is also called an arc.

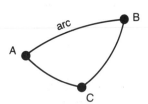

### Area
A measure of the amount of surface. We measure area in square units like the square inch ($in^2$) or square centimetre ($cm^2$) or square metre ($m^2$).

### Average
One number which represents a set of numbers. Usually when people talk about an average they are referring to the arithmetic *mean*. Other averages are the *median* and the *mode*.

## Axis
The *horizontal* number line of a graph is called the *x*-axis. The *vertical* number line is called the *y*-axis. The *x*-axis and *y*-axis are sometimes called *coordinate* axes. The point where the axes cross is the *origin*.

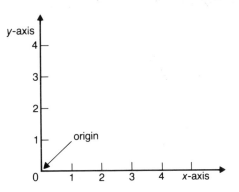

The line about which a *figure* is *symmetrical* is called an axis of symmetry, a line of symmetry or a mirror line.

Axis of symmetry

## C

## Cancelling
Making a *fraction* simpler by dividing both top (*numerator*) and bottom (*denominator*) by the same number. See also *simplest form*.

## Capacity
The capacity of a container is the amount of space inside it.

## Centimetre
$\frac{1}{100}$ of a metre. There are 10 *millimetres* in 1 centimetre (1 cm).

## Centre
The centre of a circle is the point from which the *circumference* of the circle is always the same distance. The distance from the centre to the circumference is called the *radius*.

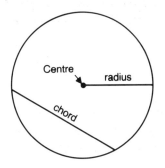

## Chord
A straight line joining two points on a circle. A *diameter* is the longest chord of a circle.

## Circumference
The measure of the distance around a circle.

## Clockwise
The direction in which the hands of a clock travel.

## Column(s)
An arrangement of numbers or letters placed one above the other. In a table of numbers or letters, columns are up and down the page, **rows** are across.

| x | 1 | 2 | 3 | 4 | 5 |
|---|---|---|---|---|---|
| 1 | 1 | 2 | 3 | 4 | 5 |
| 2 | 2 | 4 | 6 | 8 | 10 |
| 3 | 3 | 6 | 9 | 12 | 15 |
| 4 | 4 | 8 | 12 | 16 | 20 |
| 5 | 5 | 10 | 15 | 20 | 25 |

Row

Column

## Common fraction
A *fraction* whose *numerator* is smaller than its *denominator*, Examples $\frac{1}{4}$, $\frac{2}{3}$, $\frac{3}{5}$ are common fractions (sometimes called 'proper fractions').

## Compass

In geometry, an instrument used to draw a circle or arc of a circle. It is sometimes used to mark off equal lengths.

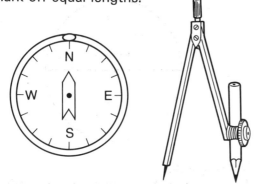

Compass is also the name of an instrument used to find direction, e.g. north.

## Concave

In geometry, shapes which point in or curve in on themselves are said to be concave. A concave *quadrilateral* is shown in the diagram. See also *convex*.

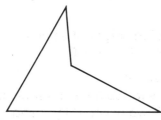

## Congruent

In geometry, *figures* that are the same in all respects are called congruent. They are the same size and shape. The example shows congruent triangles.

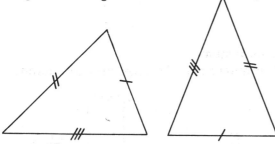

## Consecutive

Numbers are consecutive when they follow on from each other without leaving any numbers out. For example, the numbers 3, 4, 5 are consecutive.

## Convert

To change from one form into another. For example, if we convert $\frac{1}{2}$ into a decimal fraction we get $0 \cdot 5$.

## Convex

In geometry, these are shapes which point out, or curve out, rather than in on themselves. See also *concave*.

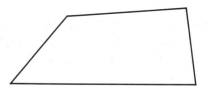

## Coordinate

On a graph, we need two numbers to find the position of a point. The order in which we write and use the two numbers is important and they are called an ordered pair for this reason. Such points are called coordinates. In the diagram for point P, 3 is the $x$-coordinate and 2 is the $y$-coordinate. We write this as (3, 2).

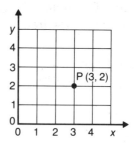

## D

## Data

Facts given sometimes as numbers, charts or graphs.

## Decagon

A *polygon* with ten sides.

## Decimal
Means based on ten or tenths.

## Decimal point
A dot or point that separates the *decimal fraction* from whole numbers.

## Decimal fraction
Any *fraction* may be written in decimal form. Example $\frac{3}{4}$ is $0 \cdot 75$ as a decimal fraction. Usually people call these simply 'decimals'.

## Degree
In geometry, a degree (°) is the unit we use for measures of turn. There are 360° in a whole turn. The right-angle is 90°.

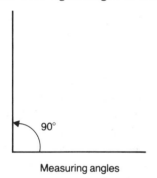

Measuring angles

In temperature measurement a degree is a unit of temperature. Example 0 °C is the temperature at which water freezes.

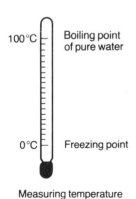

Measuring temperature

## Denominator
In *fractions*, the number below the line which gives the number of parts. In $\frac{3}{4}$, 4 is the denominator and 3 is the *numerator*.

## Diameter
A *chord* which passes through the *centre* of a circle.

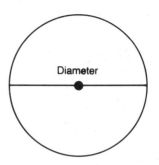

Diameter

## Difference(s)
The amount by which one quantity or number is bigger or less than another. The mathematical sign which tells us to find the difference between two numbers is the subtraction or minus sign.

## Digit
Any of the numbers 0, 1, 2, 3, 4, 5, 6, 7, 8, 9. The number 18 has the digits 1 and 8.

## Digit sum
The sum of the digits of a number. The digit sum of 18 is $1 + 8 = 9$.

## Divide, division
This means to separate into *equal* parts. For example, if we divide 8 by 2 and get 4, we have separated 8 into 2 equal parts of size 4. **Division** is the inverse, or opposite, of *multiplication*. For example $18 \div 6 = 3$ and $6 \times 3 = 18$.

## E

## Enlargement
This means to make larger in size or number.

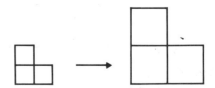

## Equal

The same amount. *Angles* are equal if they measure the same. Masses are equal if they weigh the same. The symbol for equal is =.

## Equilateral

Having sides of the same length. An **equilateral triangle** has all its sides equal and all its angles equal.

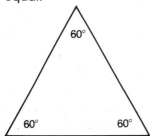

## Equivalent fractions

These are fractions with the same value. Examples $\frac{1}{2} = \frac{2}{4}$, $\frac{1}{3} = \frac{2}{6}$. See also *cancelling*.

## Estimate

When we judge the size, number or value of something, we call it an estimate. See *approximate* and *rounding*.

## Exact(ly)

Without any amount left over. When buying something, we might try to give the exact amount of money. When dividing numbers and there is no *remainder* we could say e.g. $15 \div 3 = 5$ so 3 goes into 15 by an exact amount or 3 goes into 15 exactly.

## F

## Factor(s)

3 and 5 are factors of 15 because they both *divide* into 15 *exactly*, with no *remainders*.

## Figure

Usually we mean a geometrical diagram of a triangle, square, circle, sphere, cube, etc.

Sometimes any drawings, such as those in this book, are called figures.

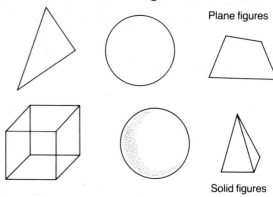

Written digits are also called figures.

## Fraction

See *common fraction, equivalent fraction, improper fraction*.

## H

## Hexagon

A *polygon* with six sides.

## Horizontal

A horizontal line on a page is one which goes across the page.

## Hundredth

Written sometimes as $\frac{1}{100}$th, this means one of a hundred equal parts. It can also mean the last of a hundred items.

## I

## Image

See *object*.

## Improper fraction

A fraction in which the *numerator* is bigger than the *denominator*. Examples $\frac{4}{3}, \frac{10}{8}, \frac{11}{5}$. Also called top-heavy fractions.

## Increase

Make larger in size or number.

## Integer

Whole numbers such as −1, 0, 3, 4, 11.

## Isosceles trapezium

A trapezium with two opposite sides equal in length. It also has two sets of equal angles.

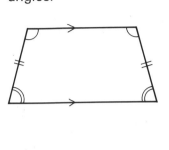

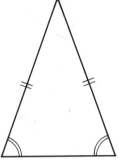

## Isosceles triangle

A triangle with two sides the same length, and two equal angles.

## K

### Kilometre

1000 metres. See *metric*.

### Kite

A quadrilateral with one pair of equal sides joining at one end and another pair of equal sides joining at the other. The diagonals of a kite cross at *right-angles*. It has only one *line of symmetry*.

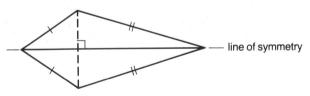

line of symmetry

### Knot

A speed of 1 *nautical mile* per hour.

## L

### Last digit

In an integer such as 123, the last digit is 3. It tells us the number of ones (units).

### Length

The measure from one end to the other of a line or object gives its length. There are many units of length, e.g. *millimetre, centimetre*, metre, *kilometre*, inch, foot, yard, mile.

### Line graph

A drawing which shows information on a graph by points joined with lines.

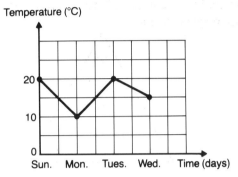

### Line of symmetry

The line about which a *figure* is *symmetrical*.

## M

### Mean

The mean is found by dividing the sum of the items by the number of items. It is often referred to as 'the average'.
Example: The mean of 6, 8 and 10 is
$$\frac{6 + 8 + 10}{3} = 8$$

### Measurement

The size or amount of something. Examples *length* may be measured with a ruler or tape; *angles* may be measured with a protractor.

A measurement has a number followed by a unit: a plank may be 3 metres (3 m) long; the angle between two walls may be 90 degrees (90°).

All measurements are approximations (see *approximate*).

### Median

A type of *average*. The median is the value in the middle after a list of numbers or measurements has been arranged in order. The median of  2  3  4  7  9 is 4.

in the middle

When the list has an even number of items, the median is the *mean* of the two values in the middle. The median of

1  3  5  7  8  9  is  $\dfrac{5 + 7}{2} = 6.$

in the middle

## Metric

Comes from the word **metre**, which is the standard measure of length. The metric system is a system of measures based on the metre, the litre and the gram. Smaller and larger units are decimal fractions, and multiples by ten, of these.

| Milli | Centi | Deci | Metre <br> Litre <br> Gram | Kilo |
|-------|-------|------|------|------|
| $\frac{1}{1000}$ | $\frac{1}{100}$ | $\frac{1}{10}$ | | 1000 |
| | Smaller | | | Larger |

## Millimetre

One thousandth of a metre. We shorten millimetre to mm.

$1\text{ mm} = \frac{1}{1000}\text{ m}$      $10\text{ mm} = 1\text{ cm}$

## Million

One thousand thousand, written 1 000 000. Remember that the word million has seven letters and the number 1 000 000 has seven digits.

## Mixed number

A number which is partly a whole number and partly a fraction. Examples  $2\frac{1}{2}$   $1\frac{3}{4}$  $10\frac{9}{10}$

## Mode

A type of *average*. The mode is the most 'popular' value – the item which occurs most frequently. The mode of 2  6  3  2  2  7  1 is 2 – it occurs more frequently than any of the other numbers. Sometimes there is more than one mode. The modes of 2  4  6  1  6  2  7 are 2 and 6.

## Multiplication

A quick way of adding lots of the same numbers together. When three fives are added together we may write 5 + 5 + 5 = 15. This addition is the same as 5 × 3 = 15, and is read as five multiplied by three equals fifteen.

15 is the *product* of this multiplication.

## N

## Nautical mile

A measure of length used at sea. It is longer than a land mile. Approximately 1 nautical mile is 1·15 land miles.

## Negative numbers

Numbers less than zero, written −1, −2, etc. Temperature scales sometimes show negative and *positive* numbers.

## Network

A pattern of connected lines.

## Node

A point in a *network* where *arcs* meet. A, B, C and D are nodes.

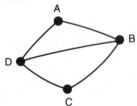

## Nonagon

A polygon with nine sides.

## Numerator

The number above the line in a *fraction*. It tells us how many of the kind of fraction there are. Example   the 4 in $\frac{4}{5}$ tells us there are *four* fifths.

## O

## Object

When you look at yourself in a mirror, you are the object and what you see in the mirror is your **image**. In geometry the shape which is being reflected is called the object. See also *reflection*.

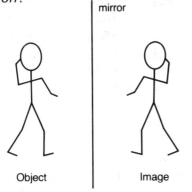

mirror

Object        Image

## Obtuse angle
An obtuse angle is an angle greater than 90°, but less than 180°.

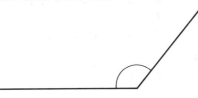

## Octagon
A polygon with eight sides.

## Operation keys
These tell a calculator what to do with any numbers fed into it.
Example 3 $\boxed{+}$ 4 $\boxed{=}$ 7. Here the $\boxed{+}$ key is the operation key which tells the calculator to add 4 to 3.
$\boxed{-}$, $\boxed{\times}$ and $\boxed{\div}$ are other operation keys.

## Origin
The point of intersection of the $x$- and $y$-axes on a graph. The origin has the coordinates (0, 0).

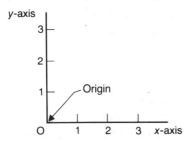

**P**

## Palindromic number
A number which reads the same when the digits are read backwards or forwards.

Example    1 7 3 7 1   forwards / backwards

## Parallel
Parallel lines never meet, no matter how far they are extended. Railway lines are parallel. The shortest distance between parallel lines is always the same. In geometry, arrows are used to show that lines are parallel.

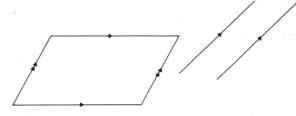

## Parallelogram
A *quadrilateral* formed by two pairs of *parallel* lines.

## Pentagon
A *polygon* with five sides.

## Percentage
A fraction whose *denominator* is 100.
Examples   $\frac{20}{100}$ may be written 20% (20 per cent);
$\frac{1}{2} = \frac{50}{100} = 50\%$.

## Perimeter
The length of the boundary of a shape.
Example   the perimeter of this triangle is 4 cm + 4 cm + 3 cm = 11 cm.

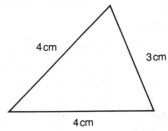

The perimeter of a circle is its *circumference*.

## Pictogram

A chart showing information by means of picture symbols that represent a certain amount.

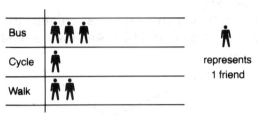

How my friends go to school

## Pie-chart

A way of representing information by dividing up a circle.

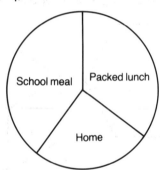

**Form 2C at lunch time**

## Plane

A flat surface.

## Polygon

A many-sided *plane* shape whose sides are all straight lines. Examples:

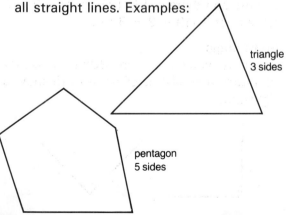

triangle
3 sides

pentagon
5 sides

## Positive numbers

Numbers greater than zero. They may be written +1, +2, +3, or simply 1, 2, 3. See also *negative numbers*.

## Product

The result of a multiplication. Example 24 is the product of 4 and 6 (4 × 6 = 24).

## Proper fraction

See *common fraction*.

## Protractor

An instrument used for measuring *angles* or for drawing angles accurately. Some protractors are circular.

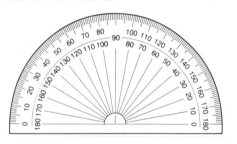

## Q

## Quadrilateral

A *polygon* with four sides. Examples of quadrilaterals are a *trapezium*, *kite*, *parallelogram*, *rectangle* and *square*.

## Quarter

A fourth part, usually written $\frac{1}{4}$. Example $\frac{1}{4}$ hour = 15 minutes.

## R

## Radius

The distance from the *centre* to any point on the *circumference* of a circle.

## Rectangle

A special kind of *parallelogram* with all its angles equal to 90°.

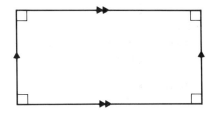

## Rectangular numbers

Whole numbers which can be shown as a pattern of dots in the shape of a rectangle.

Examples:   $6 = 3 \times 2$   •  •  •
                              •  •  •

$12 = 4 \times 3$   •  •  •  •
                              •  •  •  •
                              •  •  •  •

## Recur

To happen over and over again. A digit or group of digits may be repeated endlessly in a *decimal fraction*. We call this a **recurring decimal**.

Example:   $\frac{1}{3} = 0 \cdot 333\,33 \ldots$

We write this with a dot over the first 3 in the decimal $\frac{1}{3} = 0 \cdot \dot{3}$ and say it as 'zero point three recurring'.

## Reflection

The way in which an *image* is seen in a mirror when an *object* is placed in front of the mirror.

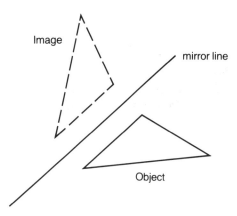

In geometry, reflection is the change of position of an object, so that the mirror line is a *line of symmetry* for the whole diagram.

## Reflex angle

An angle which measures greater than 180° but less than 360°. Angle *a* is a reflex angle.

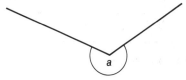

## Regular

A regular *polygon* has *equal* sides and equal angles. An example is a regular *hexagon*.

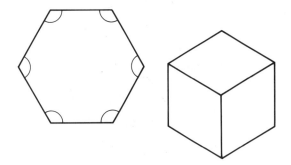

A regular solid has identical faces. A cube is a regular solid.

## Remainder

What is left over when a quantity is shared equally. When 10 sweets are shared equally between 3 people, each person has 3 sweets and there is 1 left over; $10 \div 3 = 3$ remainder 1 ($10 \div 3 = 3\,r\,1$).

## Right-angle

An angle which measures 90° or a quarter of a turn. A symbol is often used to show a right-angle.

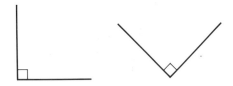

## Rounding

This is writing a number or a measurement in a special way. We do this because the number might not be exact (like the length of a line) or to make the number easier to read or remember.

A number can be rounded to the nearest whole number, nearest 10, nearest 100 and so on.
Money can be rounded to the nearest £.
Length can be rounded to the nearest cm or m.

e.g. 47 to the nearest 10 is 50
315 to the nearest 100 is 300
£1·72 to the nearest £ is £2

When the quantity is exactly half-way we usually round up.

e.g. £2·50 to the nearest £ is £3
50 cm to the nearest m is 1 m

## Row

See *column(s)*.

## S

## Scale

The scale of the model is 1 to 100.

Real car

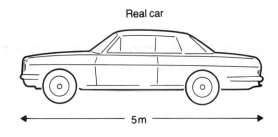

5m

Model car

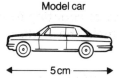

5cm

A scale on a straight line or curve helps us to measure. The marks on the scale are usually the same distance apart.

Temperature is measured with a thermometer marked in degrees. Length may be measured with a ruler marked in mm.

## Scalene triangle

A triangle whose sides are all different in length and whose angles are all different in size.

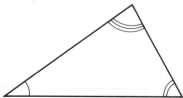

## Semi-circle

Half a circle. It is the shape formed by *diameter* and an *arc* of half the *circumference*.

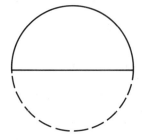

## Sharing

Means to separate into parts. For example, 12 shared into 3 equal parts is 4, or 12 ÷ 3 = 4. When the quantity to be shared cannot be shared into equal parts, the amount left over is called the *remainder*

e.g. 15 ÷ 2 = 7 r 1.

## Simplest form
Means making a fraction as simple as possible by dividing both the *numerator* and *denominator* by the same number.

## Speed
The distance travelled in a unit of time, e.g. 30 miles in 1 hour, written 30 m.p.h.

## Square
A *quadrilateral* with all sides equal and all angles *right-angles* (90°).

## Square number
A whole number made by multiplying another whole number by itself.

e.g. 49 is a square number because
$$7 \times 7 = 49$$
144 is a square number because
$$12 \times 12 = 144$$
1 is a square number because
$$1 \times 1 = 1$$

Square numbers can be arranged into a square of dots.

1
●

4
● ●
● ●

9
● ● ●
● ● ●
● ● ●

16
● ● ● ●
● ● ● ●
● ● ● ●
● ● ● ●

## Statistics
The part of mathematics which studies *data*. Originally facts and figures about the state, e.g. number of farms, area of land used for crops, number of soldiers, and so on.

## Sum
The result of adding two or more quantities together. The mathematical sign used is +. Example the sum of 2, 3 and 4 is
$$2 + 3 + 4 = 9.$$

## Survey
Means to look at something to find out facts (data). You can look for the facts yourself or ask questions. For example, a survey of how pupils in your class travel to school means finding out how each pupil travels and putting your facts in a chart or as a graph.

## Symmetrical
Usually means a shape that can be divided into equal parts by a mirror line or by folding.

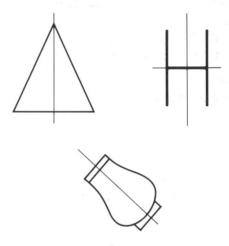

There are many other kinds of symmetry which you will learn about later.

T

## Tally
This is a way of counting by making marks. We usually make the marks into 'bundles' of fives.

||||  ||||  ||      the tally is 12

## Tenth

When something is separated into 10 equal parts, a tenth or $\frac{1}{10}$ is one of the parts.

One tenth ($\frac{1}{10}$) of £1 is 10p.

One tenth ($\frac{1}{10}$) of 1 cm is 1 mm.

You can write a tenth as $0\cdot1$.

## Tessellation

Covers a surface with shapes joined together leaving no gaps. Here is a tessellation of *regular hexagons*. The pattern would fill the page if it were continued.

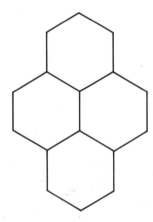

## Thousandth

When something is separated into 1000 equal parts, a thousand or $\frac{1}{1000}$ is one of the parts.

One thousandth ($\frac{1}{1000}$) of 1 kg is 1 g.

One thousandth ($\frac{1}{1000}$) of 1 km is 1 m.

You can write a thousandth as $0\cdot001$.

## Trapezium

A *quadrilateral* with one pair of sides *parallel*. We use the symbol ⇀ to show which sides are parallel.

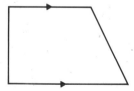

## Triangular numbers

Numbers that can be arranged into a triangle of dots.

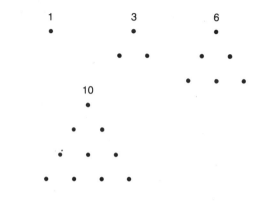

## V

## Vertical

At right-angles (90°) to the *horizontal*. Upright walls on buildings are vertical.

## W

## Width

In a rectangle is the distance from side to side, usually measured from a long side to a long side.

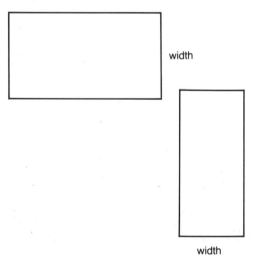

width

width